Lead Belly
no stranger to the blues

Lead Belly Archives

the songs of
Huddie Ledbetter

Selected from the historic
field research of
John A. Lomax and Alan Lomax
Original recordings of the Library of Congress,
ARC, Capitol Records, Musicraft, RCA Records
and Smithsonian Folkways Records

Music Transcriptions
(from Lead Belly's Original Recordings)
by **Harry Lewman**

TRO **Folkways Music Publishers, Inc.**

Lead Belly Honors

1949
Oklahoma Folklore Society, Award of Merit.

1972
Inducted into the National Academy of Popular Music/Songwriters' Hall of Fame in New York City.

1980
Inducted into the Nashville Songwriters' Hall of Fame in Nashville, Tennessee.

1983
Fannin Street area in Shreveport, Louisiana renamed "Ledbetter Heights".

1988
Inducted into the Rock and Roll Hall of Fame in Cleveland, Ohio.

1991
Inducted into the Louisiana Hall of Fame, Bossier City, Louisiana.

1994
Life-size statue of Lead Belly by sculptor J. Pitts, Jr. erected in Shreveport, LA.

1998
Lifetime Achievement Award from the Folk Alliance in Memphis, Tennessee.

Lead Belly Archives

To learn more about Lead Belly please consider joining The Lead Belly Society, which circulates a quarterly publication entitled the Lead Belly Letter. For more information contact: The Lead Belly Society, PO Box 6679, Ithaca, NY 14851

Lead Belly Archives

...During his most successful years, Lead Belly was considered a folk singer, not a blues singer. His reputation as a folk singer was justly deserved but in some measure resulted from the material he was asked to record. The temper of those times — late 1930s to late '40s — and of the men who recorded him, was perhaps more suited to songs that reinforced prevalent liberal political thought (Lead Belly was the darling of the old Left) than to those that spoke of sexuality, infidelity, bad women and repentant men. But, **Lead Belly was no stranger to the blues.**

Don DeMichael, 1973

Lead Belly speaks about the blues...

Now I'll tell you about the blues.
All Negroes like blues. Why?
Because they was born with the blues.
Sometimes they don't know what it is.

Lead Belly, 1943

Photo by: Jack L Feibush Lead Belly Archives

Lead Belly Archives

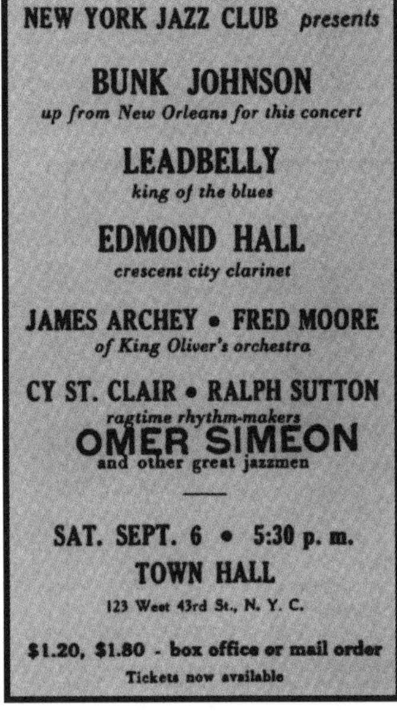

Poster for 1947 New York concert

...Never was a white man had the blues, in them times, nothin' to worry about,
But the colored man, in them times, there was hardship.
Workin', gettin' up in the mornin' 'fore day, and lay down at night about 9, 10 o'clock
Feedin' horses, milkin' cows, drivin' up the sheep, and feedin' an' callin' up the hogs every mornin',
So when the people in them times, they'd be sad and feelin' bad,
And they'd sing the blues; they didn't know how to sing nothin' else,
But, that old feelin' come to 'em. That's what they call the blues,
That old feelin'. I don't guess they knowed what they had themselves,
But they begin to sing. And they just words they would put together and sing a song,
Just a feeling, they'd make it up and they wouldn't know what they were doin' themselves, hardly,
But they just gettin' a good feelin' to 'em, see! And that's where the blues come from.

Lead Belly (Library of Congress)

Contents

Songs are in four sections in order of difficulty

Lead Belly Archives

Lead Belly is a Hard Name by Woody Guthrie

And the hard name of a harder man
The name that his mama spoke over him down in the swamps of Louisiana when he was born was Huddie Ledbettor, for her husband, Ledbettor, and because she liked the sound and the roll of Huddie.
I guess that they called him Huddie while he was growing up from dirty overhalls to knee pants, longer pants, and I've heard him sing a song about what happened to him when he did change his knee pants for his long ones
I came to his and Martha's apartment over on East Tenth Street and I carried my own guitar, and they begged me to stay, to eat, sleep, sing and dance there in their apartment of Three little rooms painted a sooty sky blue and then smoked over with the stains from cigarets, cigars, of the rich and of the poor
I saw Leadbelly get up in his morning, wash, shave, put on his bath robe, and Martha would stand up in her tall way and make me get shaved, bathed, washed, dressed, while she cooked Leadbelly his breakfast on her charcoal flat top stove. The stove was older than me, older than Martha, but not any older than Leadbelly.
I watched him set after breakfast, look down eastwards out from his window, read the Daily News and the Daily Mirror, and the Daily Worker
I listened as he tuned up his Twelve String Stella and eased his fingers up and down along the neck in the same way that the library and museum clerk touched the frame of the best painting in their gallery. It was not possible for me to count the numbers of folks that came in through Leadbelly's door there
He never did bother to count you, and Martha tried several times, but always got lost early in the morning. The people waking up in the building dropped around earliest.
Leadbelly picked along on his guitar, just something that took him back where he come from, and he played at about half of his power in order to warm up easy and to get ready for anybody that asked him for a little number on their way to hunt for coal, or for a job or work, or to a job of some kind.
I liked Leadbelly's guitar and singing this early morning speed as well, better in some ways, than the faster and stronger ones that you have seen him play on your stages and in your studios.
He had a slow running, easy, deep quiet way about him, that made me see that his strength was like a little ball in his hands, and that his thoughts ran as deep in color as the lights that played down from the sky and onto his face.
I went with Leadbelly to all kinds of places where he performed, in your school, church, your theatre, your radio studio, at your cocktail club, and at your outdoor rally to call you to come together to meet, talk, argue, theorize, and speak your voice against the things that poison your life and your world around you. I saw that what you applauded in some was diplomas, degrees, intellectual pursuit, the reading of books, the tracings of our histories, and the speakers fighting for our wages, hours, homes, union. I saw you make just as much of an applause for Leadbelly as for your other leaders, and the thing that you applauded in him was pure personal fighting power. The same power as the prisoner of War that cries and sings, dances, after he is freed from a death camp.
Leadbelly had to find every lost ounce of his strength to keep him alive down the road he has come.
He had to find it to even live and to grow up from a little boy into the full man. His street around him was rough and wild, it was dirty, worn thin, rotten, naked and hungry. It was buggy, crummy, old and wore out, it was a street of old sickly shack houses, as old, older maybe, than his daddy and his daddy's daddy. The going was tough, and the strong of wind and muscle got along a little better than the weak ones, and it helped the weak ones to fight harder, grow harder. He did not smoke tobacco, gamble, play poker, dice, nor waste his time at idle things. The artist in him was a hungry man, hungry to see himself in the best clothes, on the best street, in the best room, the best car, the best world. He knew he could help his folks everywhere to keep up their fight and their faith, if he could only win his better place. This is the feeling that he found in his soul and the feeling that he brought to the touch of his first guitar. This was the sight of the vision that he saw. This was his way. The sight and the feel of his music box in his hands lit up those homeless stretches of his spirit and he said, This is my way.
Leadbelly said, this is my way. And he said it the same, in the same airy breath that George Washington Carver said of his science laboratory. Leadbelly touched his first guitar the same tender way that Joe Louis felt the skin of those first gloves. The same as Paul Robeson first touched his football, his Shakespeare costume as Hamlet. He said, This is my way, about the same as Marian Anderson touched her throat and sang at her great places. Leadbelly did not know where his guitar would carry him, but he said that he would follow it.
His guitar was not like a friend of his, not like a woman, not like some of the kids, not like a man you know. But it was a thing that would cause people to walk over to where he is, a thing that made sounds that gave his own words richer sounds, and would give him his way to show his people around him all of the things that he felt inside and out. He would play the tones on the music box and then he would tell me a story, you a tale, and all of his life history. And he would say and sing it in such words that we could not tell where our own personal life stopped and Leadbelly's started.
He wanted to preach history, his own history, his peoples story, and everybody's history. He wanted to be all kinds of big names, a history speaker, a story teller, a talker, good fast walker, a loud yeller, and the man that was all a big tone.

Excerpt of Woody's original typed manuscript, from his book *American Folksong*, Oak Publications, Inc.

Woody Guthrie performs with Lead Belly, Chicago 1941 Photo by: Stephen Deutch Neg: 38902; Chicago Historical Society

Presented by the Lead Belly Memorial Concert Committee

Produced by Alan Lomax,
assisted by Francis Martin

Stage manager Vernon Enoch

PROGRAM

I. Ballads and Folk Songs

Sam Gary - Alan Lomax - The Varieteers
"Blues for Lead Belly", recited by Bill Robinson, accompanied by Sammy Price
Edith Allaire - Frank Warner - Tony Kraber
Rev. Gary Davis - Jean Ritchie - Oscar Brand
Tom Glazer - Prof. Harold Thompson - W. C. Handy
Woody Guthrie and Tom Paley - Lord Invader
Hally Wood - Ensemble

II. Blues

Sonny Terry - Brownie McGhee - Sticks McGhee
Billy Taylor - Dan Burley -
Brownie McGhee's "He's Gone Away" Blues.
Mary Moore, singing "Lord, I Tried."

III. Jazz and Ragtime

Bill Dillard, narrator.
Eubie Blake and his ragtime piano.
All-Star Band with Sidney Bechet, Count Basie, Bill Dillard, Billy Taylor and others.
Hot Lips Page and His Band.
Programed by George Avakian, Charles Edward Smith, Bob Maltz.

IV. Lead Belly Memorial

Voice of Lead Belly.
Introduction of Ledbetter family.
"Take This Hammer", filmstrip about Huddie Ledbetter -
Produced by Fran Dellorca, assisted by Al Helb, Irving Toorchin -
Written by Alan Lomax.
Peter Seeger and The Weavers and the Good Neighbor Chorus, Laura Duncan.

Concert accompanist, Sam Price

Photographs courtesy Sid Grossman, Van Fisher, Betty Little, Skippy Adelman, Jean Evans

PRODUCTION COMMITTEE

Naome Walsh, Arrangements
Edith Allaire
Greer Johnson
Robin Roberts
Paul Walsh

Lead Belly Archives

Instructional notes

Lead Belly almost always played a 12-string guitar. The difference between a 12-string guitar and a 6-string guitar is that a "pair" string is added to each of the strings that would normally be on a 6-string guitar. These pairs, or courses, always have strings of the same tone, separated by an octave or not. The songs in this book are presented in order of difficulty. They are organized so that the guitarist can explore a number of different key and chord positions within each group of songs of a similar skill level. The songs that separate these groups are either a cappella or non-guitar songs.

For Guitarists...

Tuning the guitar

Each score has tuning information. The notes are listed from lowest to highest. When the guitar is tuned to the stated tuning, the tablature will match the key for the musical notation. Lead Belly often tuned his guitar a fourth below standard pitch. Feel free to follow the tablature even if your guitar is tuned more sharp or flat. Lead Belly kept very tight tolerances and seldom used open tunings. Each string was tuned in pitch with its pair string, and the courses were all pitched properly apart. But often all the strings were not pitched to a perfect note. If the guitar played a note at the A 440 position, the actual note that the strings sounded might be 40 cents above or below. Solo musicians playing string instruments soon learn that there can be a significant artistic benefit gained by pitching the actual notes of the instrument above or below a "perfect" note so as to allow vocal flexibility or to take advantage of a particular tone – either fretted or open.

For guitarists accustomed to "standard" concert tuning: E A D G B E, the only difference in Lead Belly's tuning is that all strings are reduced in pitch equally so that the desired pitch is reached.

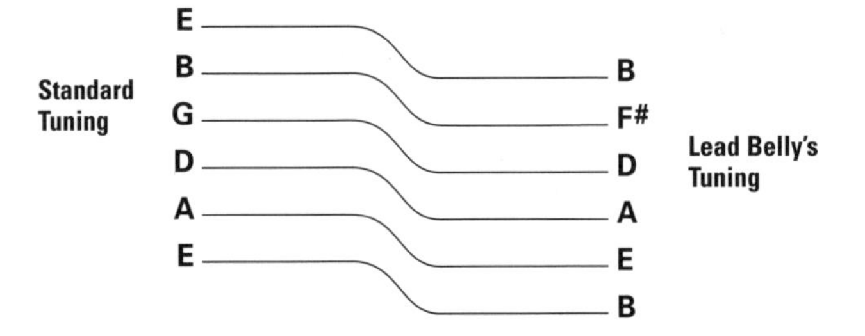

Selection of string gauges and octaves for guitar

Many of the songs have a B 2 as a bass note, that is five half-steps below standard E. In commercially available string sets of medium gauging, the low E is often a .056 diameter wound string. When tuning below this E, a larger diameter string will produce a more full, sustained tone. Lead Belly's Stella 12-string guitar (currently on loan to the Rock and Roll Hall of Fame) still has the strings that he last installed in 1949. The string gauges on Lead Belly's guitar, as measured by Bruce Taylor, are shown below. You will notice that the sixth course of strings are two octaves apart. Currently available sets usually have this course one octave apart. The third course of strings are the same octave, unlike currently available sets which have this course as one octave apart. For the well-being of the guitar, caution is advised when using larger diameter strings.

Course	*Common name*	String Gauges	Actual tuning
1st course	*High E*	.014	Note **B**
2nd course	*B*	.019	Note **F#**
3rd course	*G*	two .022 wound	Note **D**
4th course	*D*	.038; octave string .019	Note **A**
5th course	*A*	.048; octave string .019	Note **E**
6th course	*Low E*	.070; double octave string .014	Note **B**

Right Hand Technique

Lead Belly used a plastic thumb pick and an unusually long and thick metal finger pick for his index finger. He typically struck the strings with the thumb and index finger only. **In many of the songs, the thumb plays a very steady rhythm on the bass in quarter notes. These quarter notes are almost always staccato, about an eighth note duration.** Usually, his right hand dampens the string to produce the staccato effect, although it can be produced by the left hand raising off the fretboard. The bass staff closely matches the notes played by the thumb, and the treble staff has notes that would mostly be played by the index finger striking the strings.

Instructional notes

Fretting positions

Lead Belly used many standard positions, very often staying in the first position. Due to the lower pitch of the strings, it can be confusing to strum an "E" position chord which will actually produce the pitch of a B chord. (see diagram below)

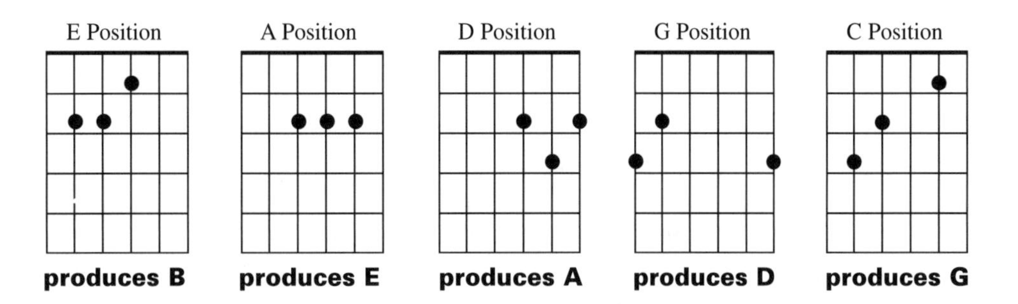

Notation and Tablature

The notation and tablature information only shows what a six-string guitar would play. The notes from the pair string have not been transcribed. This is the normal method of transcription for the 12-string guitar. The musical notation is voiced for a piano. The actual positions of the notes on the treble and bass staves are where they would sound. As per usual convention, the melody notes are written on the treble staff. The songs are scored so that the sung melody notes are exactly those of the recordings, allowing for the micro-tuning and speed anomalies that have crept into the recordings. The tablature has six lines representing the six pairs of string courses. The lowest string in the tablature will be the first note listed in the tuning information at the top of each song.

For vocalists...

Range

Lead Belly had a tenor voice that could extend well into the lyric tenor range. His range extended from an E below middle C up one and a half octaves. Many musicians have transposed the melody for their own tastes, or added embellishments. One reason that his songs have been so popular is that they are fun to sing and, in the folk tradition, amenable to improvisation.

Lyric interpretation

Lead Belly used the melody as the basis for the song structure. Many of his songs are based on folk melodies, the lyrics and the song imparting some story, or a strongly held idea. His guitar playing was secondary to his singing. Despite his prodigious talent at guitar playing, it was always his voice which was the lead instrument of the song.

For all musicians...

Tempo and rhythm

Tempo is presented in beats per quarter note per minute. Lead Belly presented his music in such a way that the listener always can ascertain a strong beat. He often played for dances and his music is rooted in the dance tradition. He usually increased the tempo of the song as he played. This was a conscious effort to impart a dynamic to the song, in the dance tradition.

Expression

Despite the strong vocal component to Lead Belly's music, his musical ideas can be well presented without vocalizing the melody. By using two contrasting instruments, a piano and a violin for instance, the full beauty and expression of the song can be well explored.

With thanks...

I would like to thank Judy Bell for her patience and knowledge, Pete Seeger for his inspiration and editing, Mark Patton and Bernie Mulleda for transcription assistance with "Silver City Bound", and Mark Davis, Sean Killeen, and Tiny Robinson.

Harry Lewman www.HLMusic.com

Where Did You Sleep Last Night?

(In the Pines) (Black Girl)

Transcribed from 1944 Musicraft sessions available on *Lead Belly/Goodnight Irene*, Tradition CD 1006. Lead Belly's Musicraft records inspired Kurt Cobain who later recorded "Where Did You Sleep Last Night?" with Nirvana on their 1994 CD *Unplugged in New York*. Other CD recordings: *Lead Belly Memorial Vols. 3 & 4* (1944 sessions originally released on Stinson label), Collectables 5604; *Lead Belly/Where Did You Sleep Last Night?* (1947 Asch sessions), Smithsonian Folkways 40044.

My girl, my girl, don't lie to me,
Tell me where did you sleep last night?
In the pines, in the pines where the sun don't ever shine,
I will shiver the whole night through.

My girl, my girl, where will you go?
I'm going where the cold wind blows.
In the pines, in the pines where the sun don't ever shine,
I will shiver the whole night through.

My girl, my girl, don't lie to me,
Tell me where did you sleep last night?
In the pines, in the pines where the sun don't ever shine,
I will shiver the whole night through.

My husband was a hard working man,
Killed a mile and a half from here.
His head was found in a driver wheel,
And his body has never been found.

My girl, my girl, don't you lie to me,
Tell me where did you sleep last night?
In the pines, in the pines where the sun don't ever shine,
I will shiver the whole night through.

(additional verses from another recording)
Black girl, black girl, don't you lie to me,
Tell me where did you sleep last night?
In the pines, in the pines where the sun never shines,
I will shiver the whole night through.

My husband was a railroad man,
Killed a mile and a half from here.
His head was found in the driver's wheel,
And his body haven't ever been found.

Black girl, black girl, where will you go?
I'm going where the cold wind blows.
You caused me to weep and you caused me to moan,
You caused me to leave my home.

Where Did You Sleep Last Night?

(In the Pines) (Black Girl)

Huddie Ledbetter

Tempo: 100 - 105

Tuning: B,E,A,D,F#,B

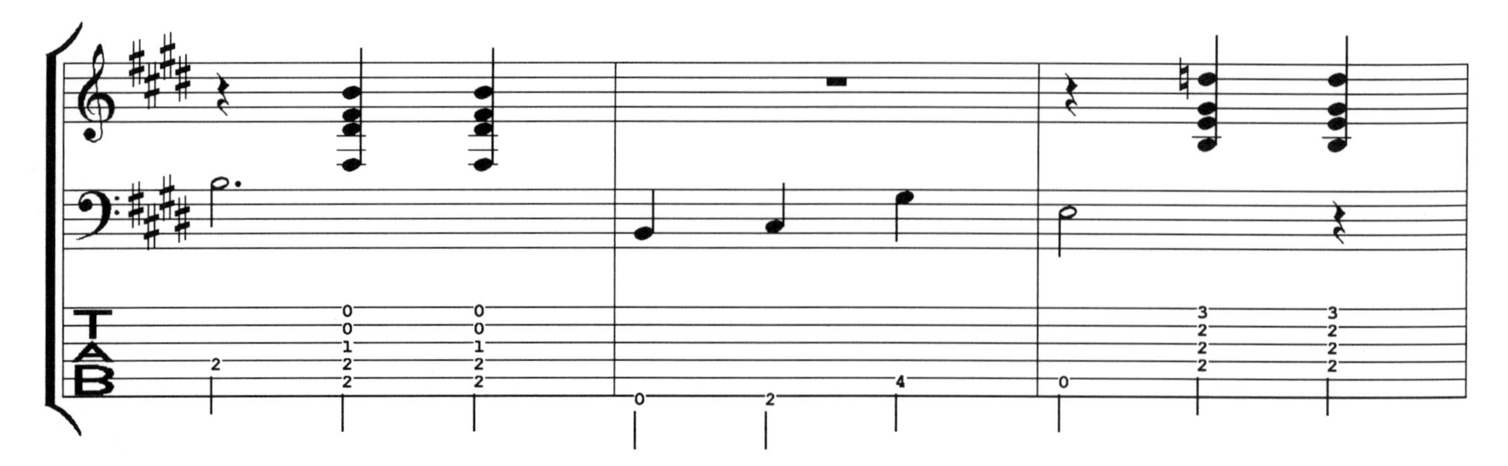

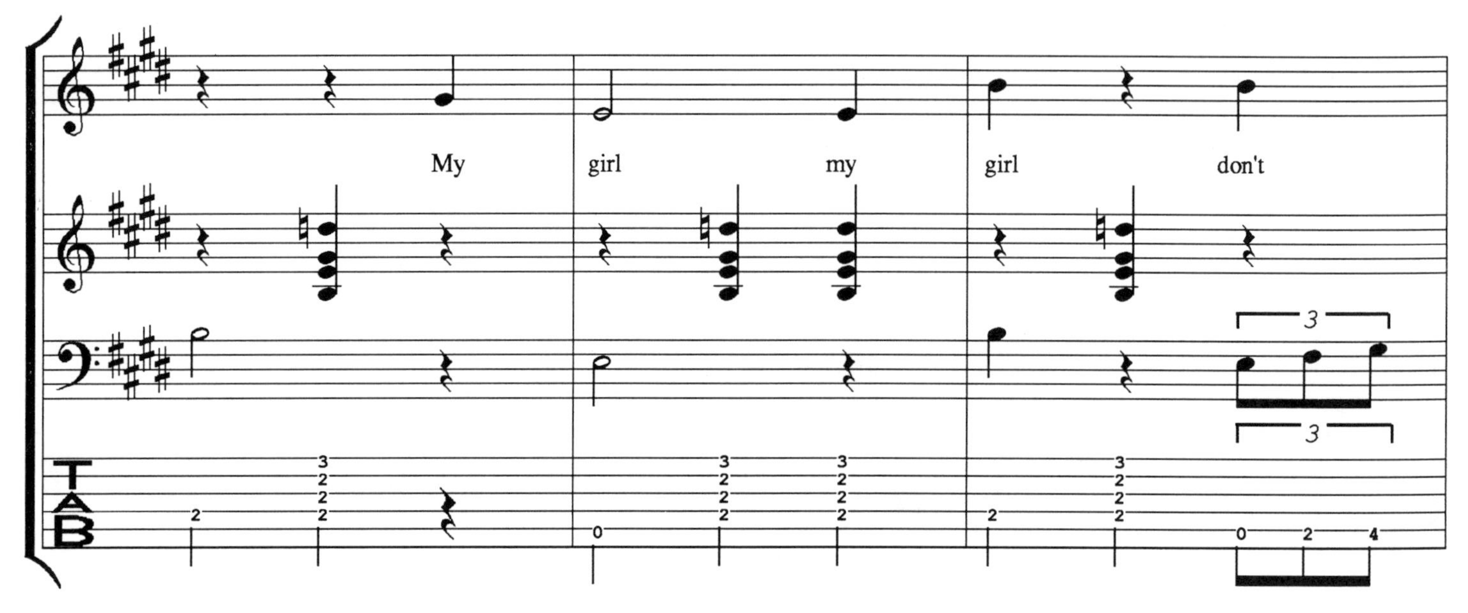
My
girl
my
girl
don't
3
3

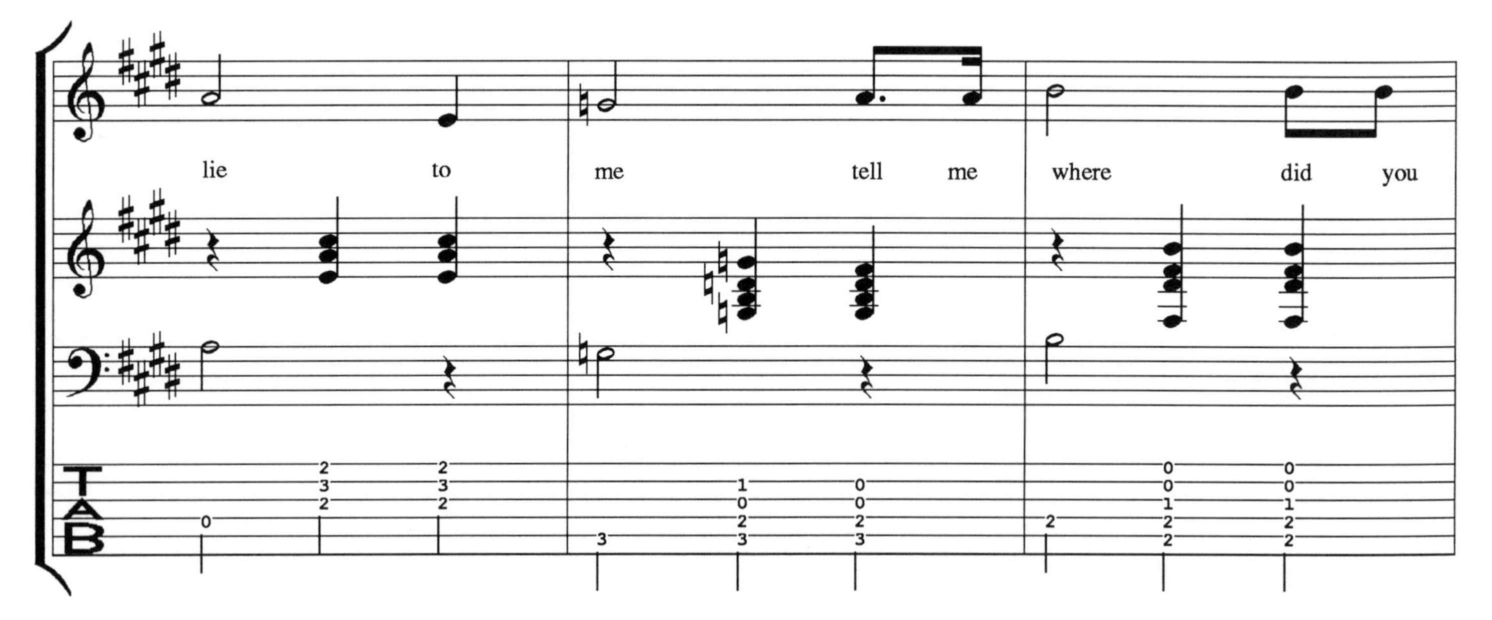
lie
to
me
tell
me
where
did
you

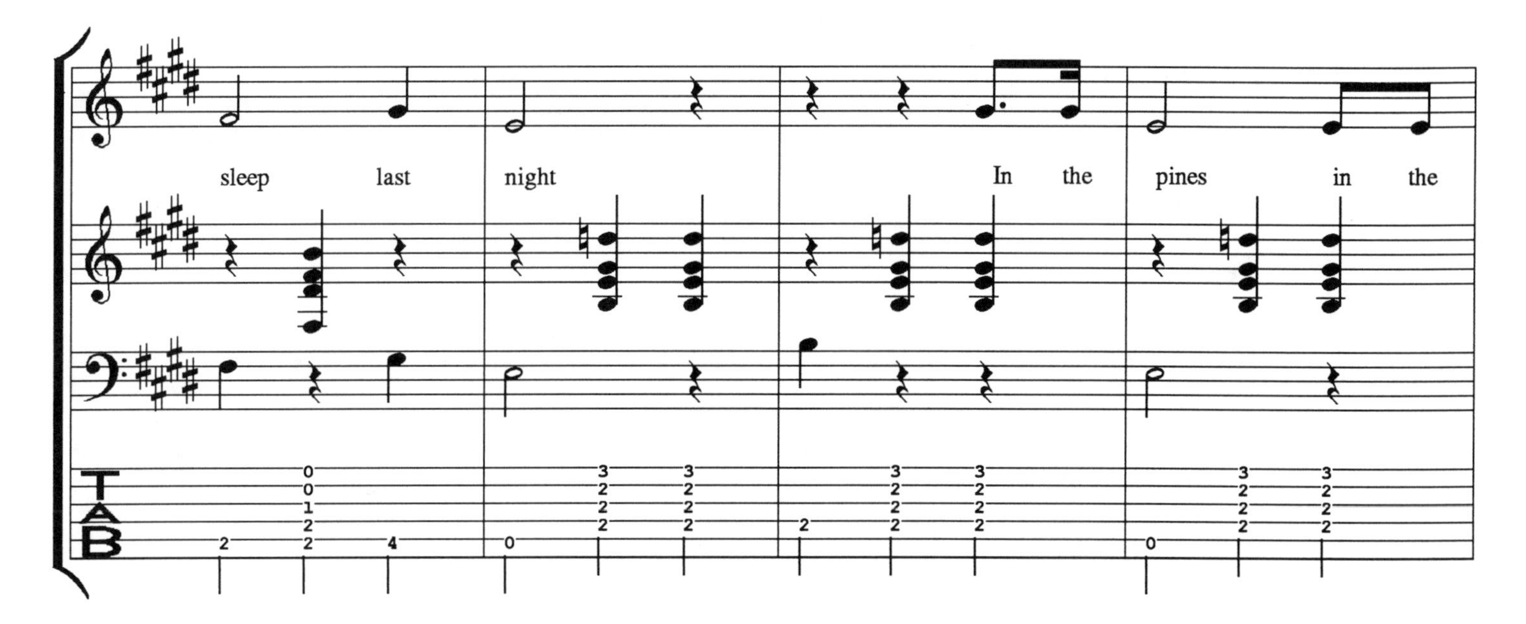
sleep last night In the pines in the

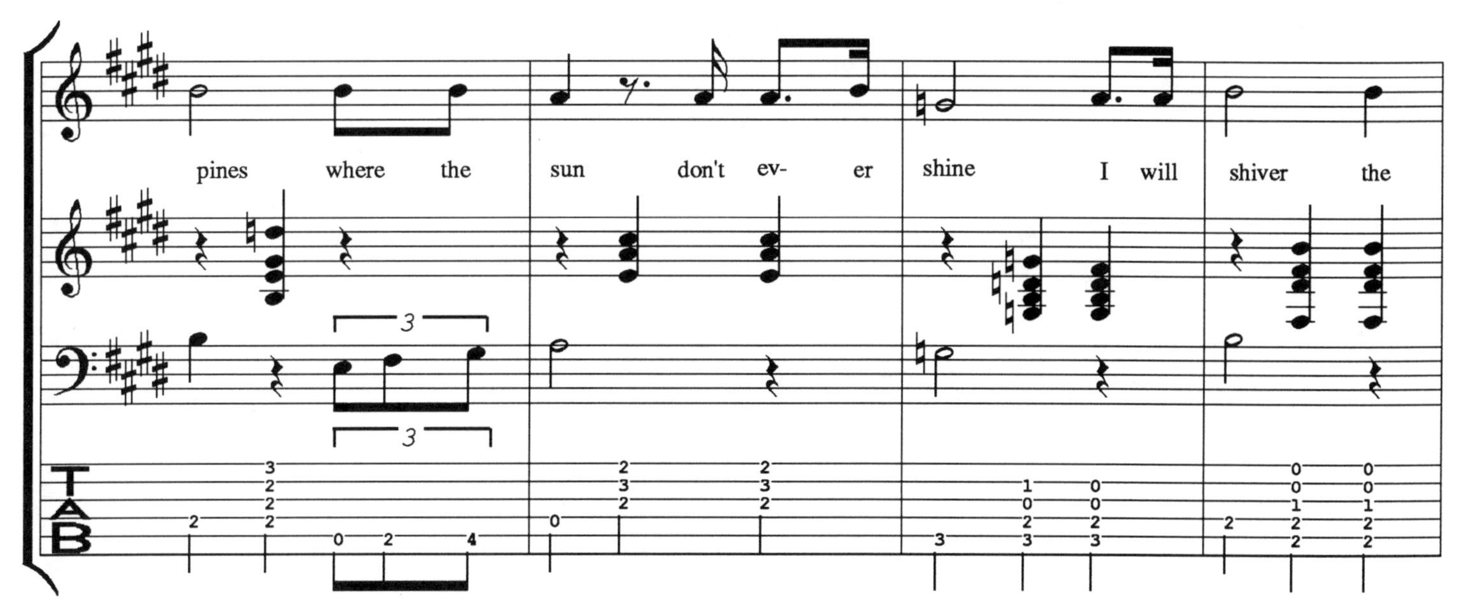
pines where the sun don't ev- er shine I will shiver the

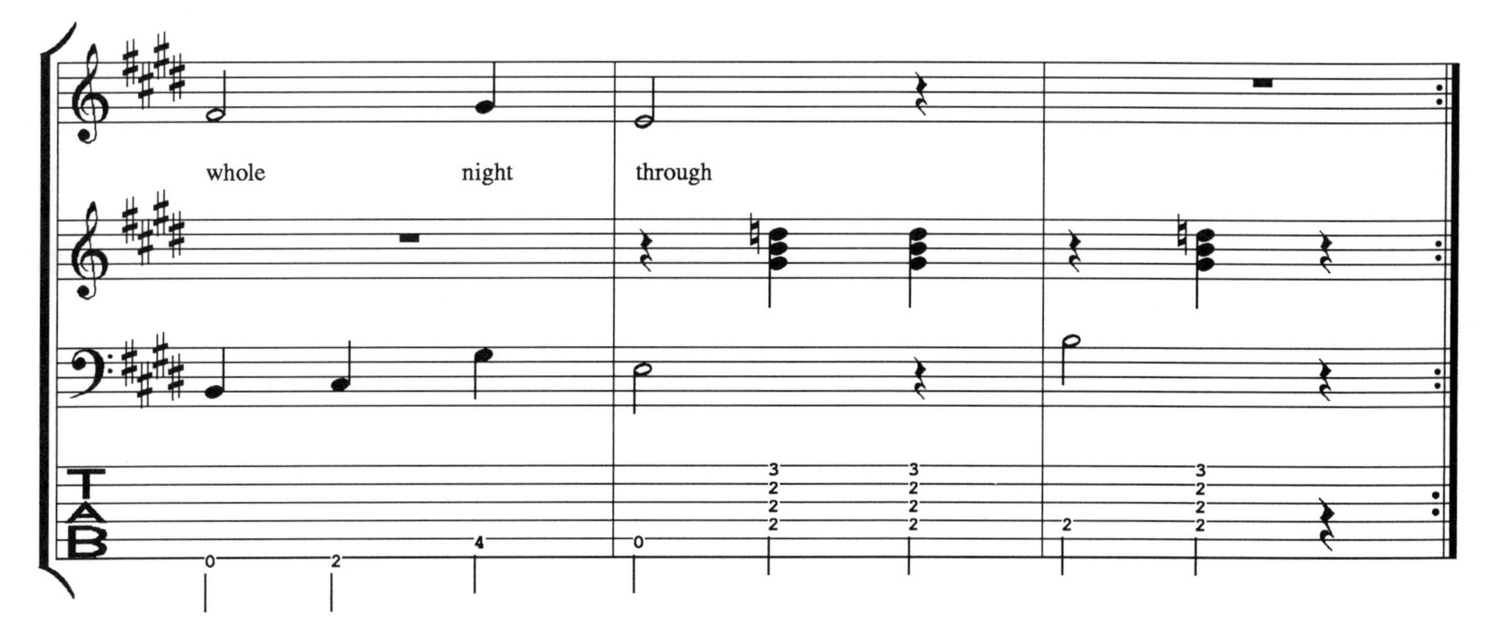
whole night through

National Defense Blues

Transcribed from 1944 Moses Asch sessions now available on *Leadbelly Sings Folk Songs*, Smithsonian Folkways CD 40010 and *Leadbelly/Defense Blues*, Collectables CD 5196. Other Lead Belly recordings: *Lead Belly's Last Sessions* (1948), Smithsonian Folkways CD boxed set 40068/71, *That's Why We're Marching/World War II and the American Folk Song Movement* (1946 previously unreleased track with assisting artists Sonny Terry, Brownie McGhee, Willie "The Lion" Smith, George "Pops" Foster), Smithsonian Folkways CD 40021.

"National Defense Blues" is one of the few songs about women who worked in the defense plants.

I had a little woman working on that national defense (2)
That woman got to the place, act like she did not have no sense.

Just because she was working, making so much dough
That woman got to the place where she did not love me no more.

Every payday come, her check was big as mine
That woman thought that defense work's gonna last all the time.

Now the defense is gone, listen to my song
Since that defense been gone that woman done lose her home.

I will tell you the truth and it's got to be the fact
Since that defense been gone that woman lose her Cadillac.

I'm gonna tell you people, tell you as a friend
I don't believe that defense will ever be back again.

National Defense Blues

Huddie Ledbetter

Tempo: 120-130

Tuning: B,E,A,D,F#,B

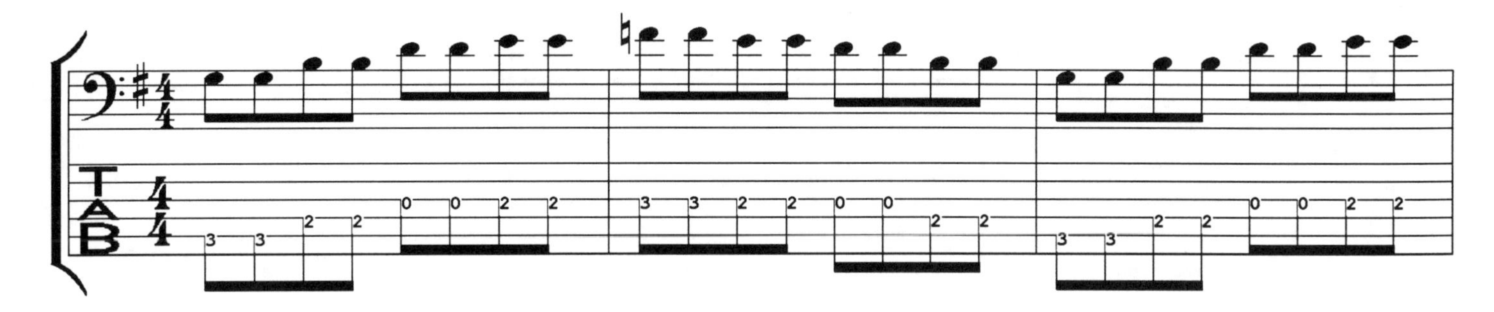

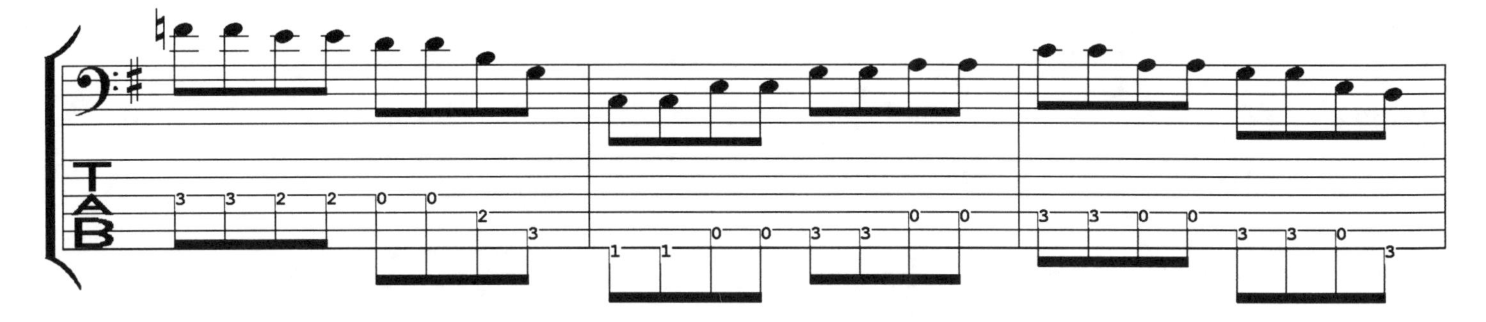

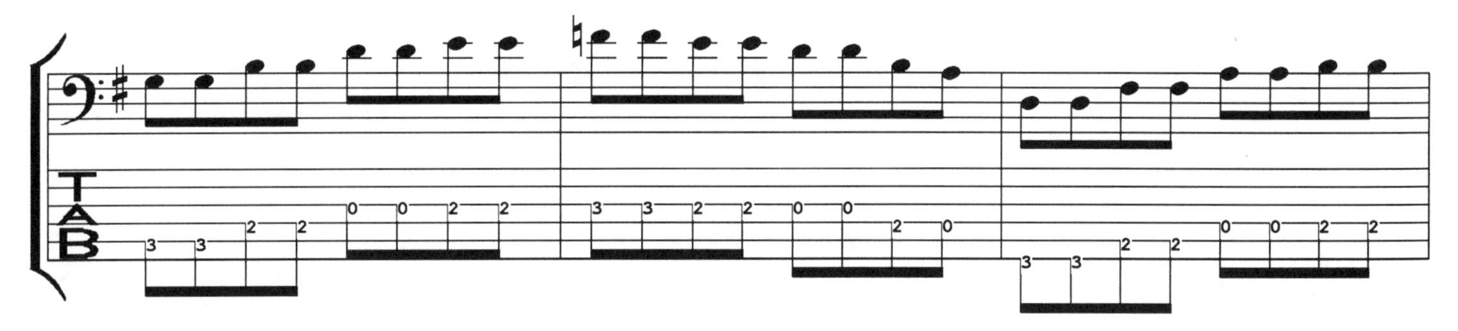

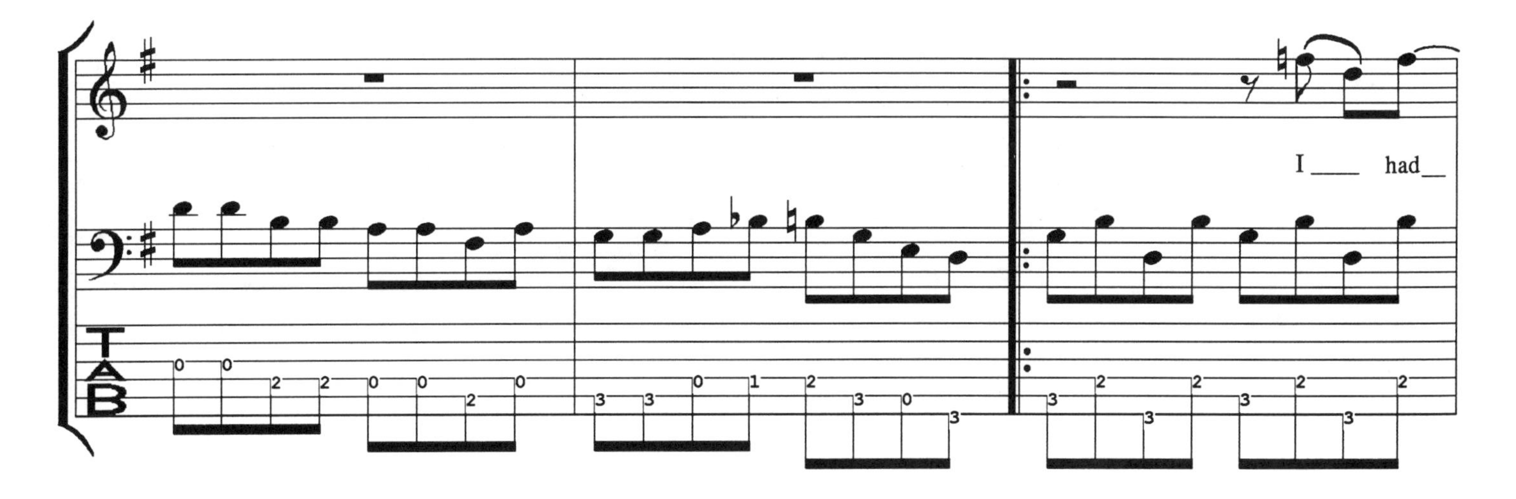

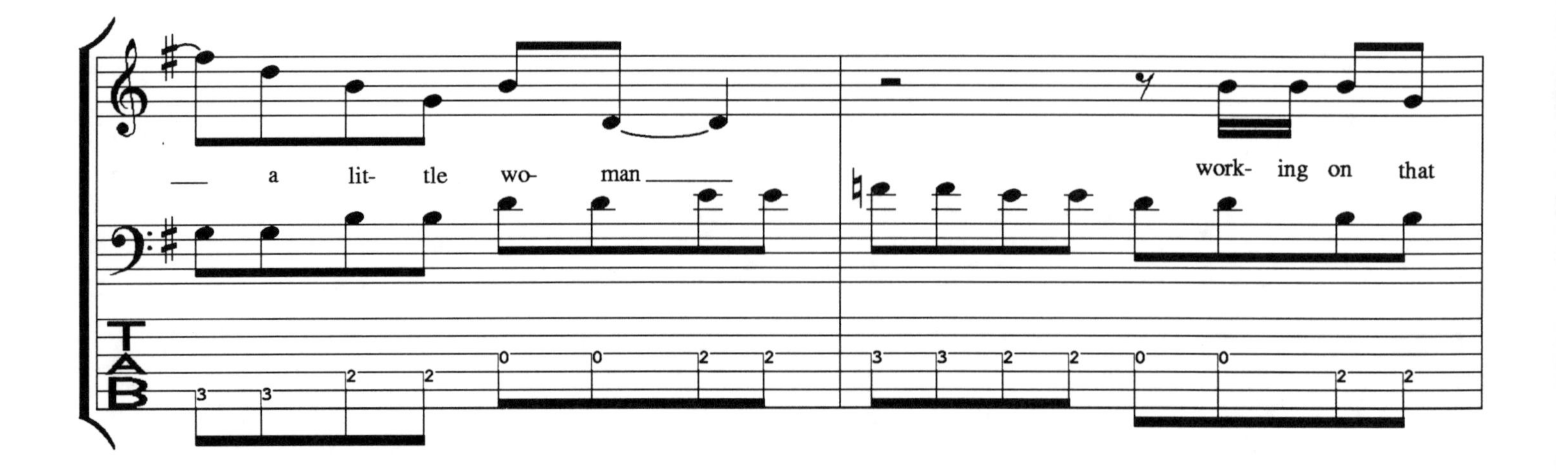
a lit- tle wo- man
work- ing on that
T
A
B

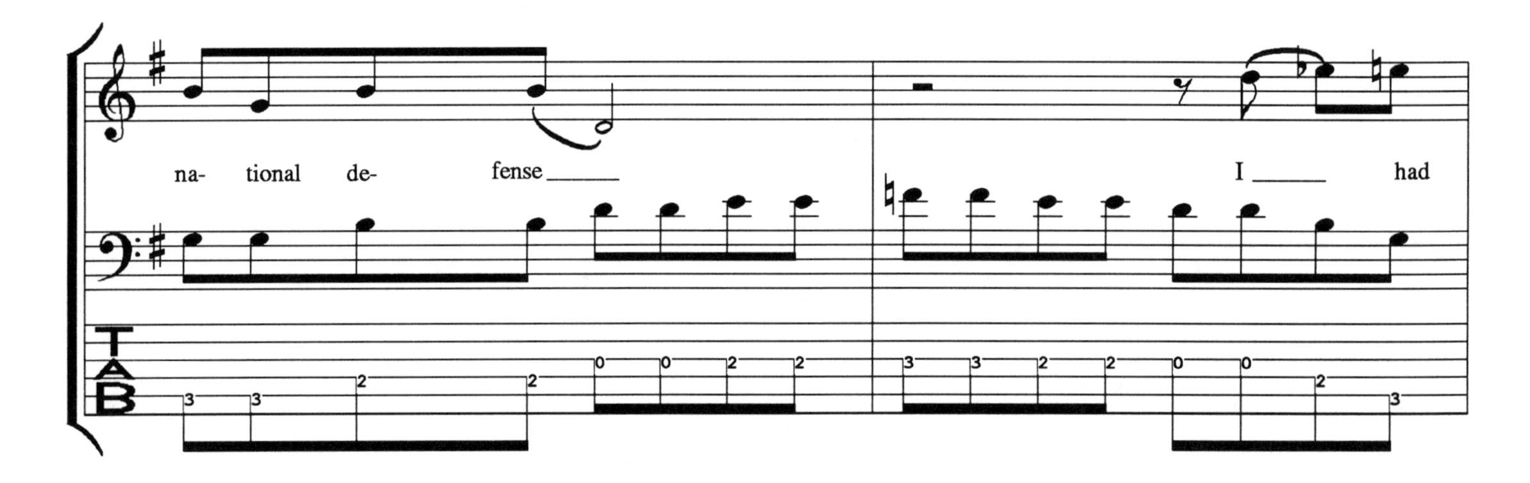
na- tional de- fense
I had
T
A
B

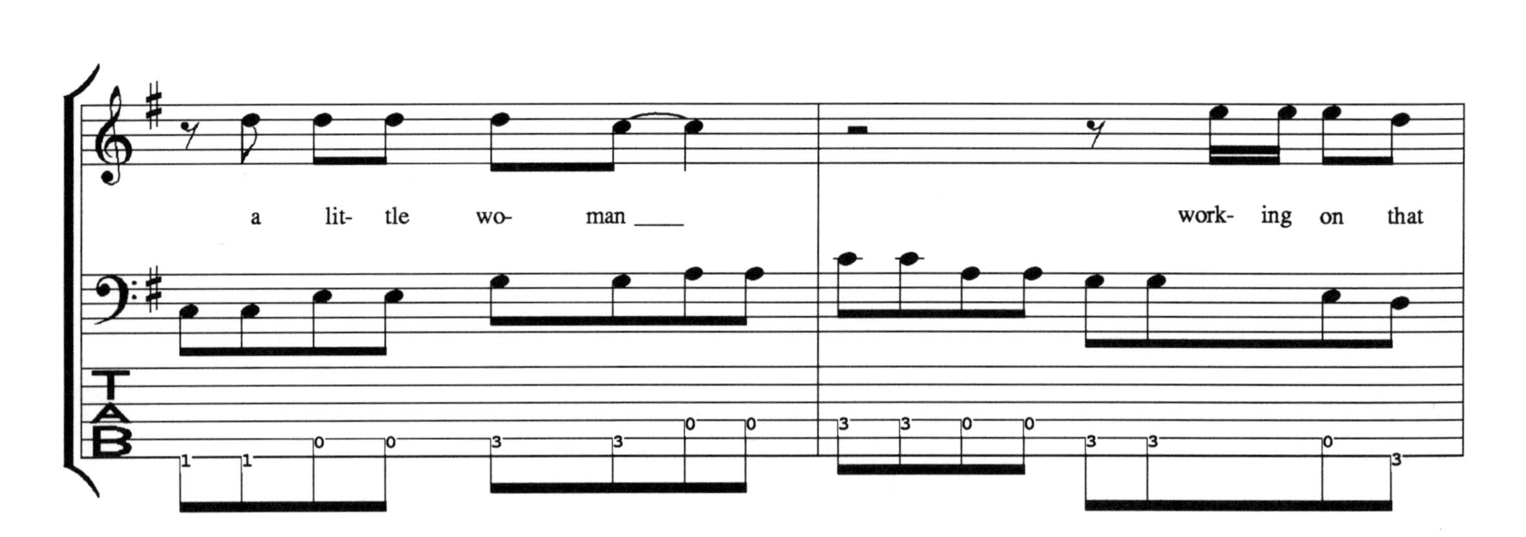
a lit- tle wo- man
work- ing on that
T
A
B

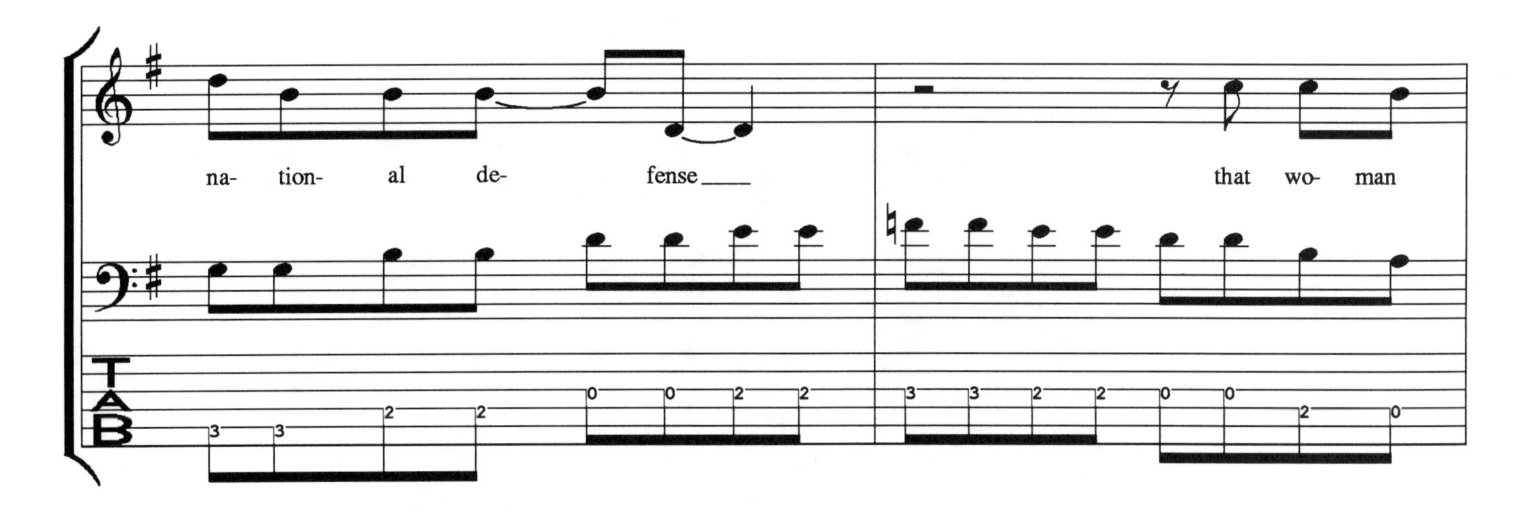

na- tion- al de- fense
that wo- man
T
A
B

3
got to the place
act like she
did not have no sense
T
A
B

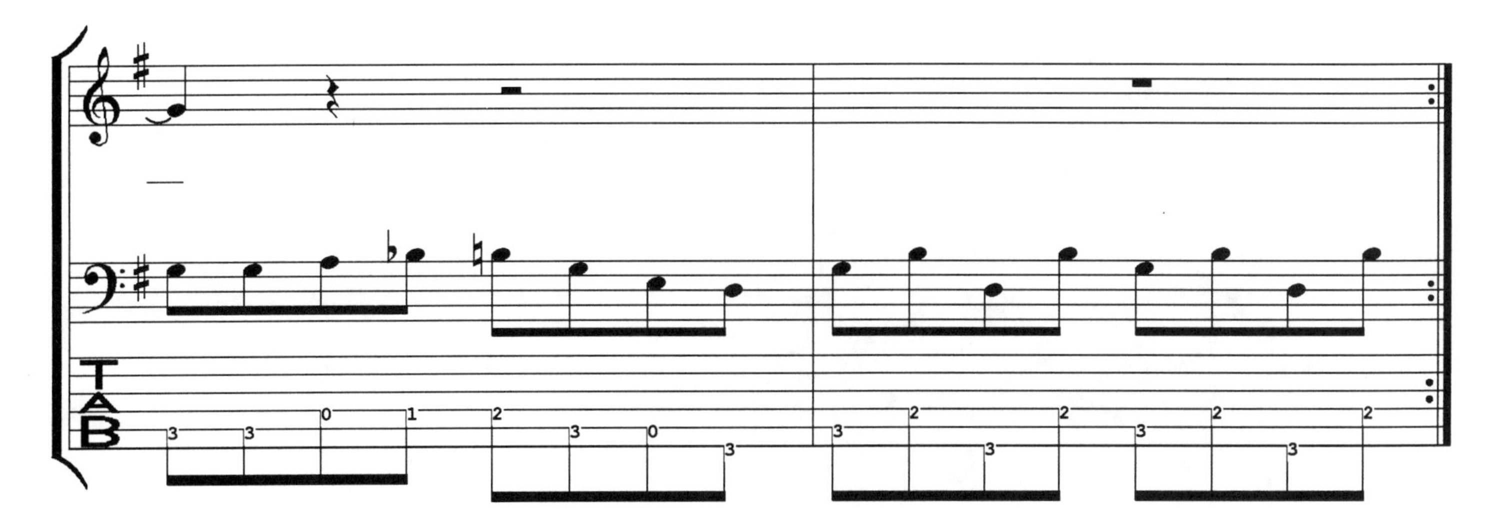

T
A
B

Lead Belly and his wife Martha, New York City, 1940s Lead Belly Archives

"We used to have what we called Blue Monday at Lead's house, and we'd sit and play - sometimes one, two, or three hours. Lead had a lot of friends he'd invite over."

- Sonny Terry

Josh White, Lead Belly and Pete Seeger, New York City, 1940s Lead Belly Archives

New York City

Transcribed from June 1940 RCA recording sessions now available on *Leadbelly/Alabama Bound*, RCA CD 9600-2-R. Another recording from 1937 Library of Congress sessions is on *Lead Belly/ Nobody Knows The Trouble I've Seen*, Rounder CD 1098.

Lead Belly and his wife Martha moved to New York City in 1936.

I'm in New York City, gonna know my line,
New York City, yes, I'm all the time.

Chorus:
In New York City, woo, ain't that a city?
New York City, believe I've got to know my line.

Well, there's one thing, folks, I ask you to do,
Catch a bus and ride up Fifth Avenue. *(Chorus)*

When you ride that bus, keep it on your mind,
Riding that bus is sure gonna cost you a dime. *(Chorus)*

When it began to get cloudy, looked like rain,
Step down inside and catch you a subway train. *(Chorus)*

Ever go down in Georgia, I'm gonna walk and talk
And tell everybody about it, the city of New York. *(Chorus)*

Ever go down in Louisiana, walk and tell,
A train run over the top of this town they call the El. *(Chorus)*

Trains run underground and they won't keep still,
Gonna catch me a train and ride to Sugar Hill. *(Chorus)*

(another verse, as remembered by Pete Seeger)
Fifth Avenue bus is the best in town,
But if you only got a nickel you got to go underground.
You really got to know your line.

New York City

Huddie Ledbetter

Tempo: 140-175

Tuning: C#, F#, B, E, G#, C#

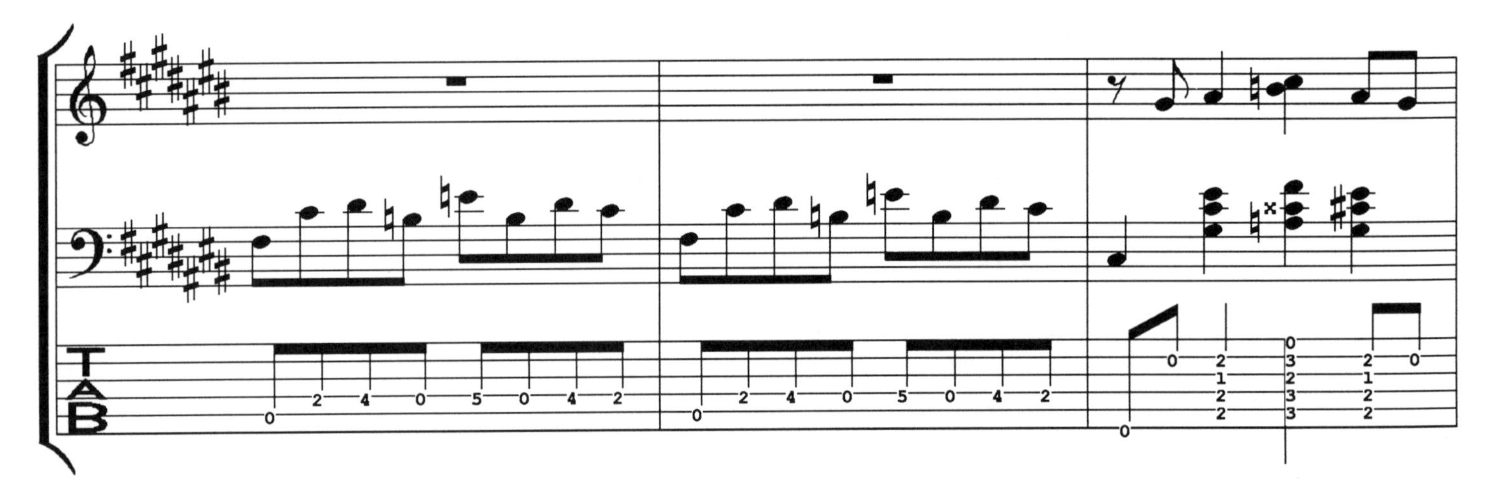

I'm in New York Ci- ty got to

know my line New York Ci- ty yes I'm all the time in
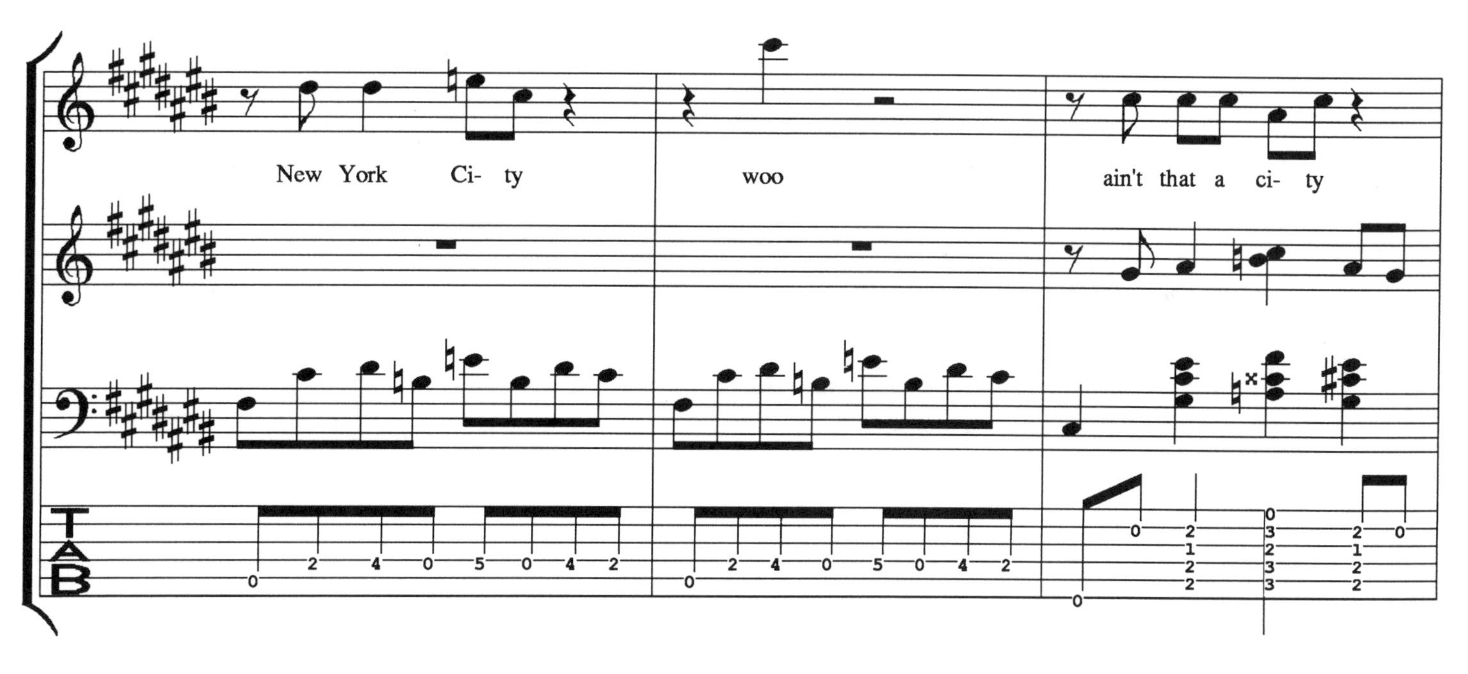
New York Ci- ty woo ain't that a ci- ty

"Lead Belly loved New York. He felt free to move about and not have to worry about someone's questioning him or a sheriff chasing him. He'd had enough of that, and he was very careful.

He had a lot of friends in New York, and he loved them all. He enjoyed playing with Pete Seeger, Woody Guthrie, Brownie McGhee and Sonny Terry, and Josh White. They were mostly kids, younger than he, but he liked the way they played banjos and guitars; and he also enjoyed playing and singing with them at hootenannies in any little hall they could find.

Lead Belly used to have a gathering of his musical friends at his home practically every night where they would all sit around on the floor and take turns playing and singing and clapping until the wee hours of the morning.

Lead Belly loved people and loved to entertain them. People were his life." Queen Ollie Robinson

Rock Island Line

Transcribed from 1942 Asch recording available on *Lead Belly/Where Did You Sleep Last Night?*, Smithsonian Folkways CD 40044. Other Lead Belly recordings: *Lead Belly/Nobody Knows The Trouble I've Seen* (1937 Library of Congress sessions), Rounder CD 1098; *Leadbelly/Alabama Bound* (1940 RCA sessions with Golden Gate Quartet), RCA 9600-2-R; *Leadbelly* (with Paul Mason Howard, zither, 1944), Capitol LP T 1821; *Folkways - The Original Vision* (1945, San Francisco - originally released on various Folkways LPs), Smithsonian Folkways CD 40001; *Lead Belly's Last Sessions* (1948), Smithsonian Folkways boxed CD set 40068/71.

The Rock Island Line was a railroad that ran between Little Rock, Arkansas and Memphis, Tennessee.

I got goats, I got sheep, I got cows, I got hogs, I got horses,
I got all livestock, I got all livestock.

(Chorus)
Oh the Rock Island Line it's a mighty good road,
Oh the Rock Island Line it's the road to ride.
Oh the Rock Island Line it's a mighty good road,
If you want to ride, you got to ride it like you find it,
Get your ticket at the station on the Rock Island Line.

Jesus died to save our sins,
Glory to God, we gonna meet Him again. *(Chorus)*

A, B, C, double X, Y, Z,
Cats in the cupboard but they don't see me. *(Chorus)*

I may be right and I may be wrong,
Know you gwine-a miss me when I'm gone. *(Chorus)*

(additional words from 1945 Folkways recording)
I fooled ya, I fooled ya, I got iron
I got all pig-iron, I got all pig-iron.

(from 1944 Capitol recording)
(spoken)
That Rock Island Line train out of Mullaine (sic)
Comin' back this way
That depot agent gonna throw that switchboard over the track
That means that Rock Island Line train's got to go in the hole
That man don't wanna stop that train
He gonna talk to the depot agent with his whistle
And this is what he gonna tell him:
(sung) I got cows, I got horses etc.
(spoken) That depot agent gonna let that train by
When that Rock Island Line train get by
That agent gonna talk back to the depot agent with his whistle
And this is what he gonna tell him,
I thank you, I thank you, I thank you
Now that little Rock Island Line train is gettin' on down the road.

Rock Island Line

Huddie Ledbetter

edited by Alan Lomax

Tempo: 95-130

Tuning: C, F, A#, D#, G, C

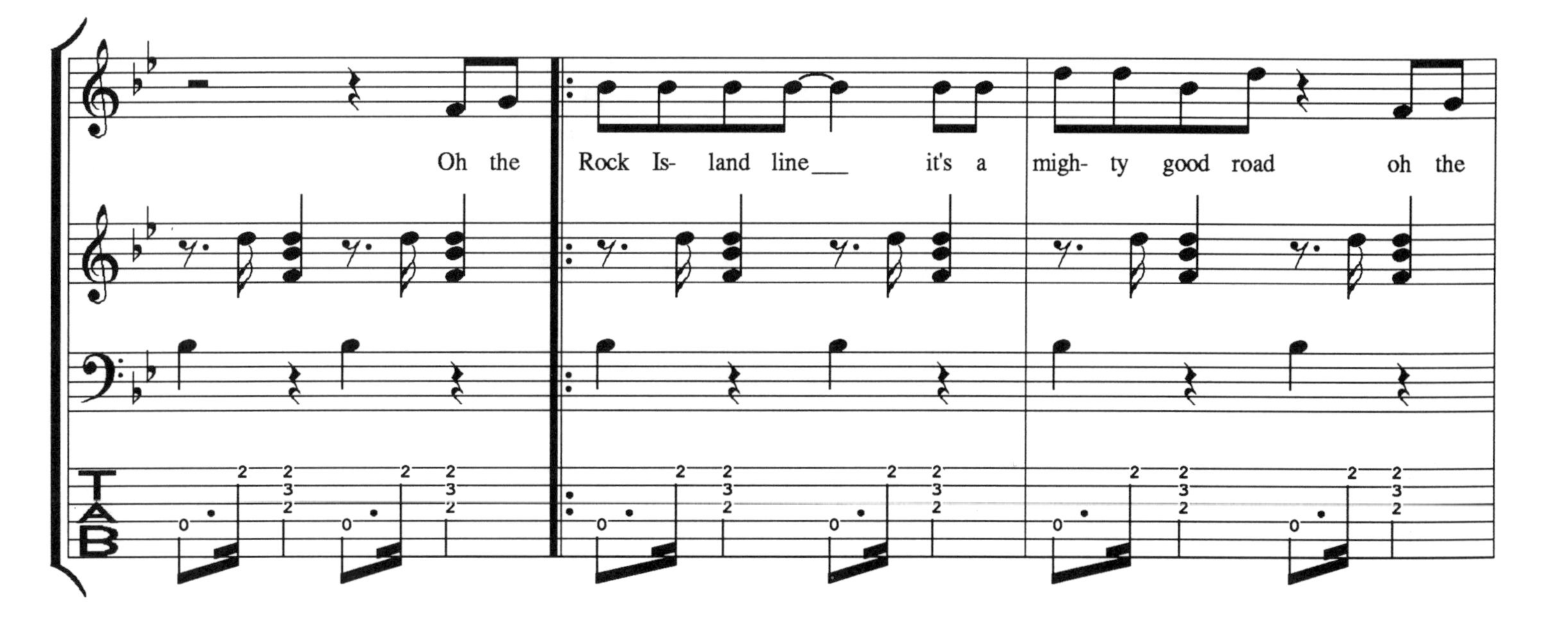
Oh the
Rock Is- land line___ it's a
migh- ty good road oh the
T
A
B

Rock Is- land line___ it's the
road to ride___ oh the
Rock Is- land line___ it's a
T
A
B

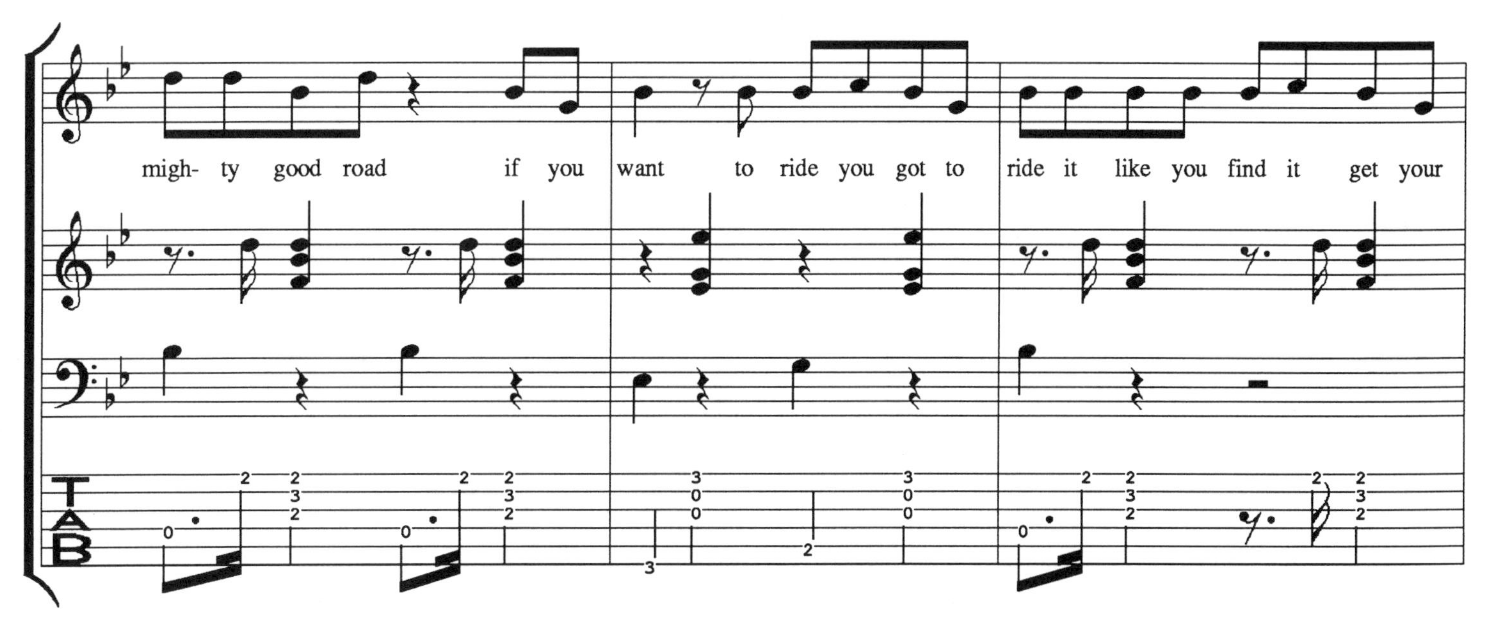
migh- ty good road if you
want to ride you got to
ride it like you find it get your
T
A
B

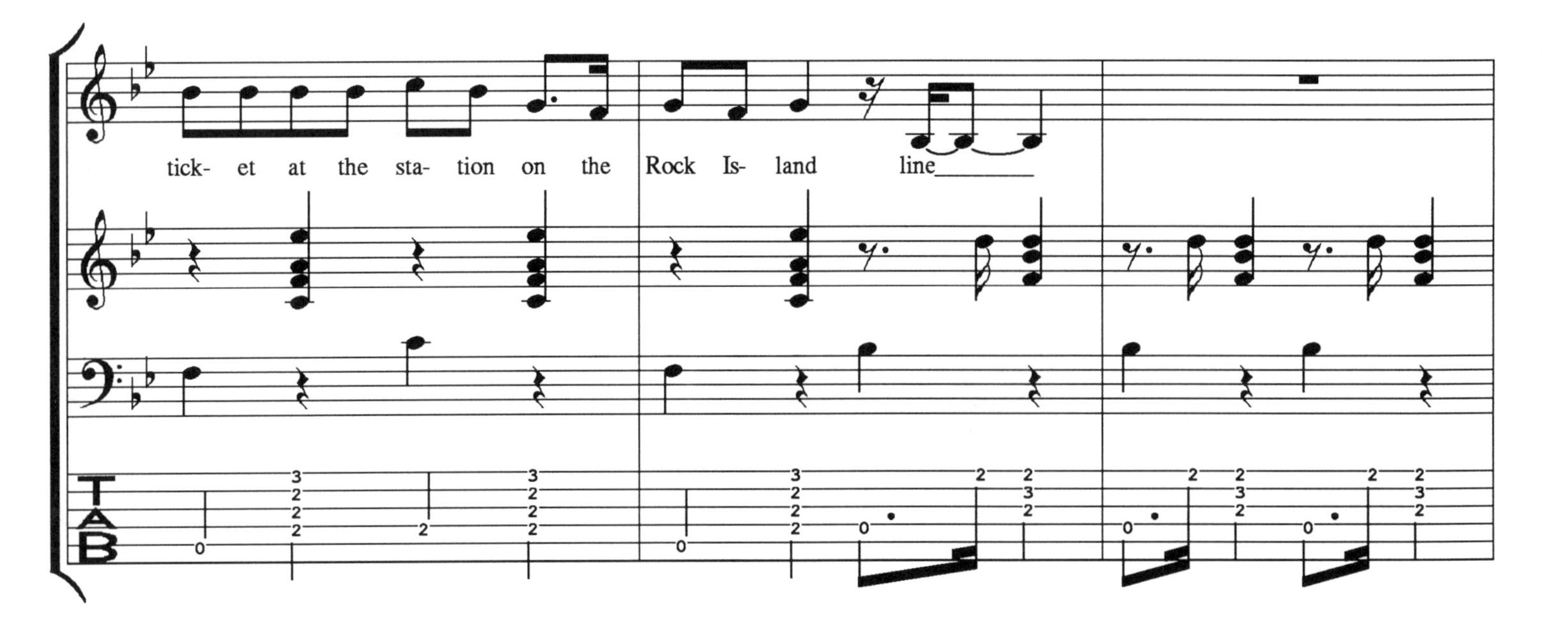
tick- et at the sta- tion on the Rock Is- land line

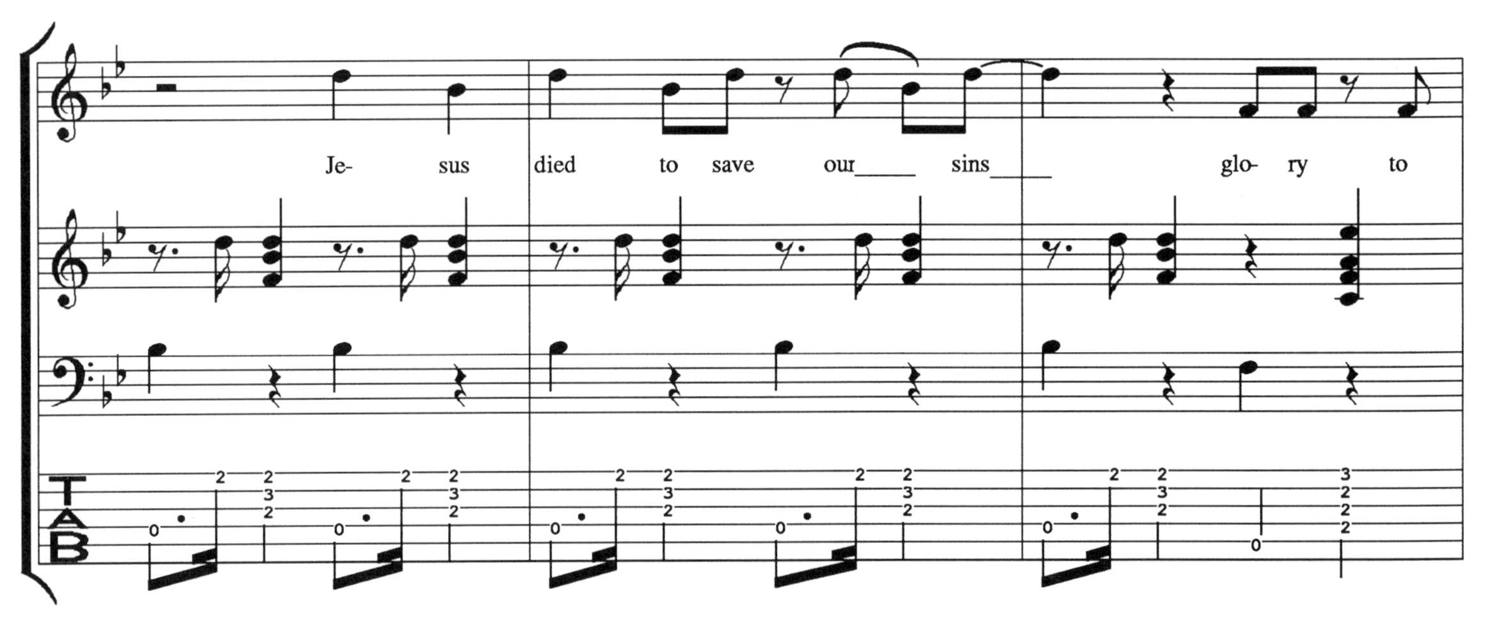
Je- sus died to save our sins glo- ry to

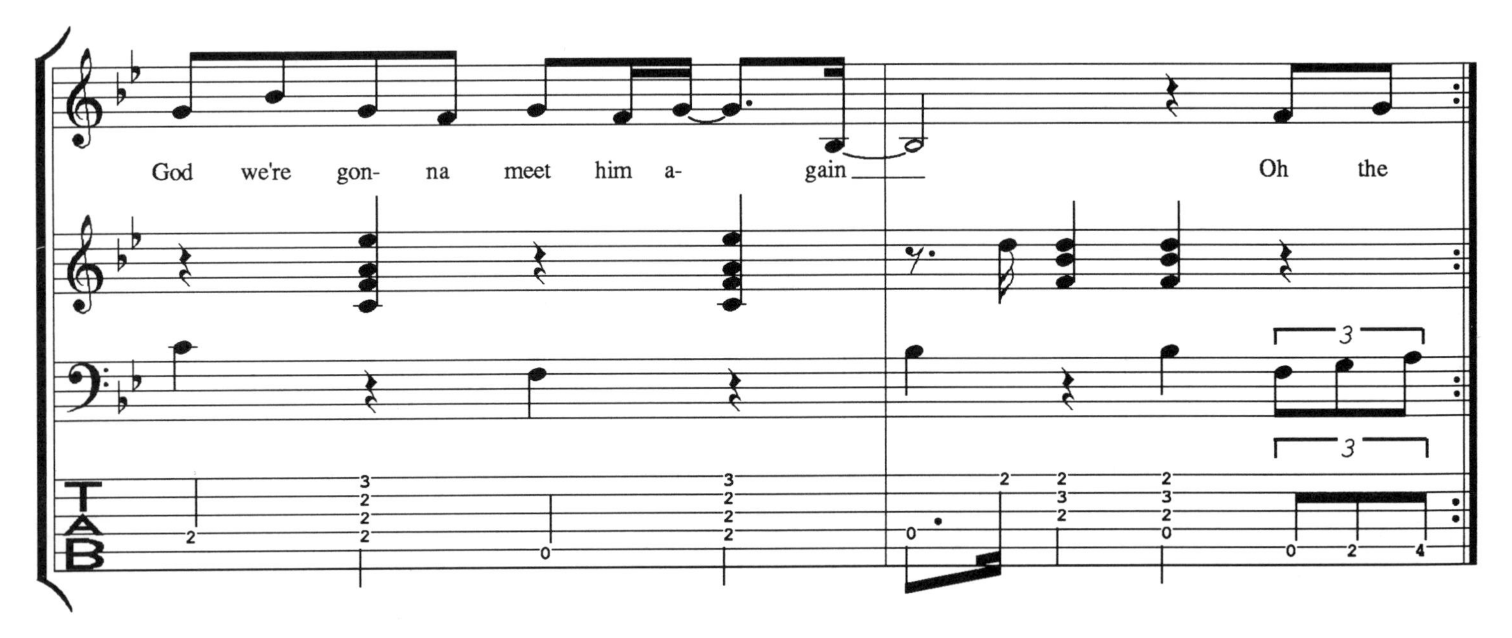
God we're gon- na meet him a- gain Oh the

Alabama Bound

Transcribed from 1946 Asch sessions with Woody Guthrie and Cisco Houston available on *Lead Belly/Bourgeois Blues*, Smithsonian Folkways CD 40045 and *Leadbelly/Party Songs & Sings and Plays*, Collectables CD 5609. Another recording: *Leadbelly/Alabama Bound* (1940 RCA sessions with the Golden Gate Quartet), RCA CD 9600-2-R.

Chorus:
I'm Alabama bound (2)
And if the train don't stop and turn around,
I'm Alabama bound.

Oh, don't you leave me here.
If you will go anyhow,
Just leave a dime for beer. (Chorus)

Elder Green is gone.
He's way 'cross this country, sweet gal,
With his long clothes on. He's Alabama bound etc.

Oh, the preacher preached,
The sisters turned around.
Yes, the deacon's in the corner hollering, sweet gal,
I'm Alabama bound. (Chorus)

The preacher's in the stand,
Passing his hands around.
He's saying, "You brothers and you sisters shoot your money to me,
I'm Alabama bound." (Chorus)

(additional verse from RCA recording)
You oughta be like me.
You can try your good high test whiskey, boys,
And let that King Corn be.

Alabama Bound

Huddie Ledbetter

Tempo: 120-135

Tuning: B,E,A,D,G,F#,B

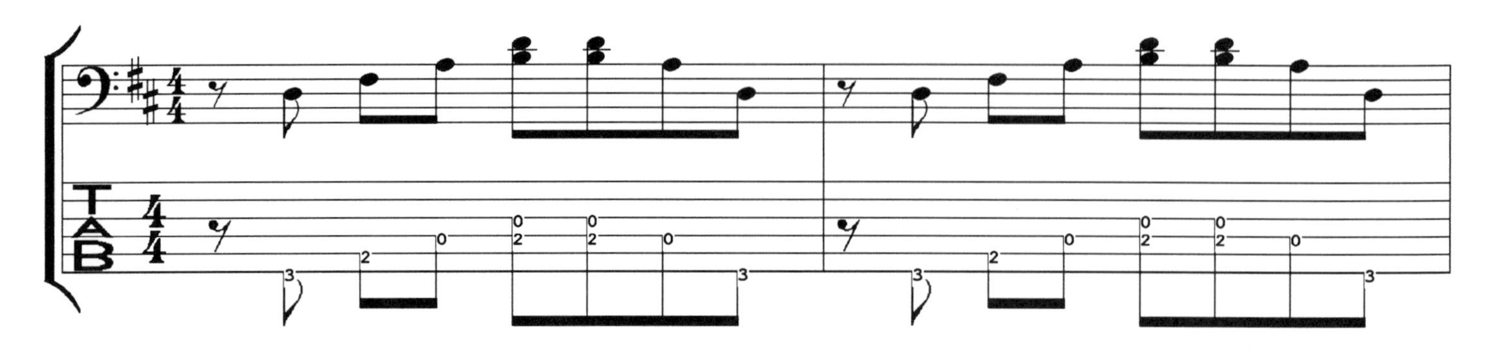

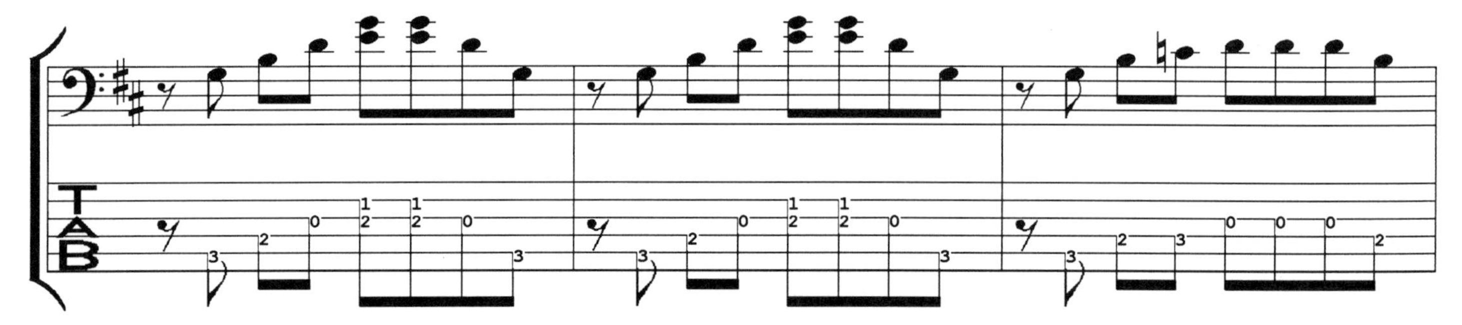

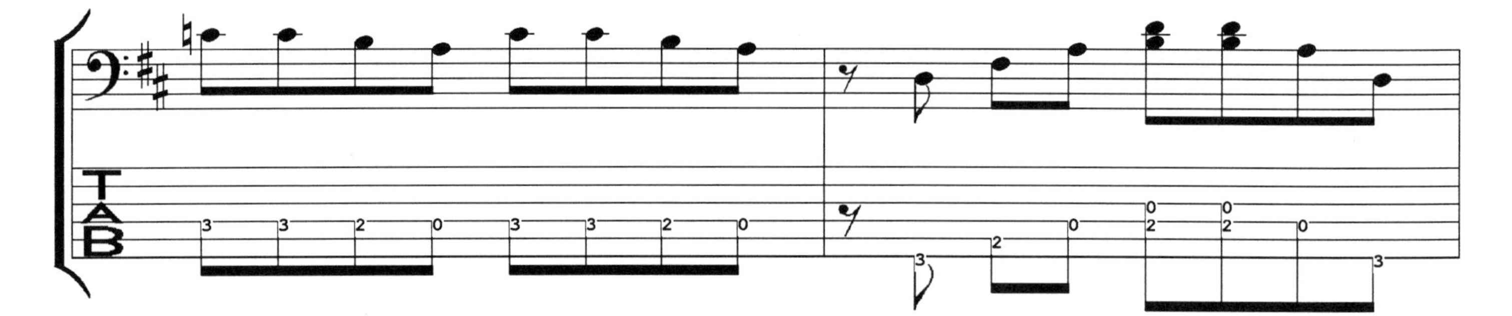

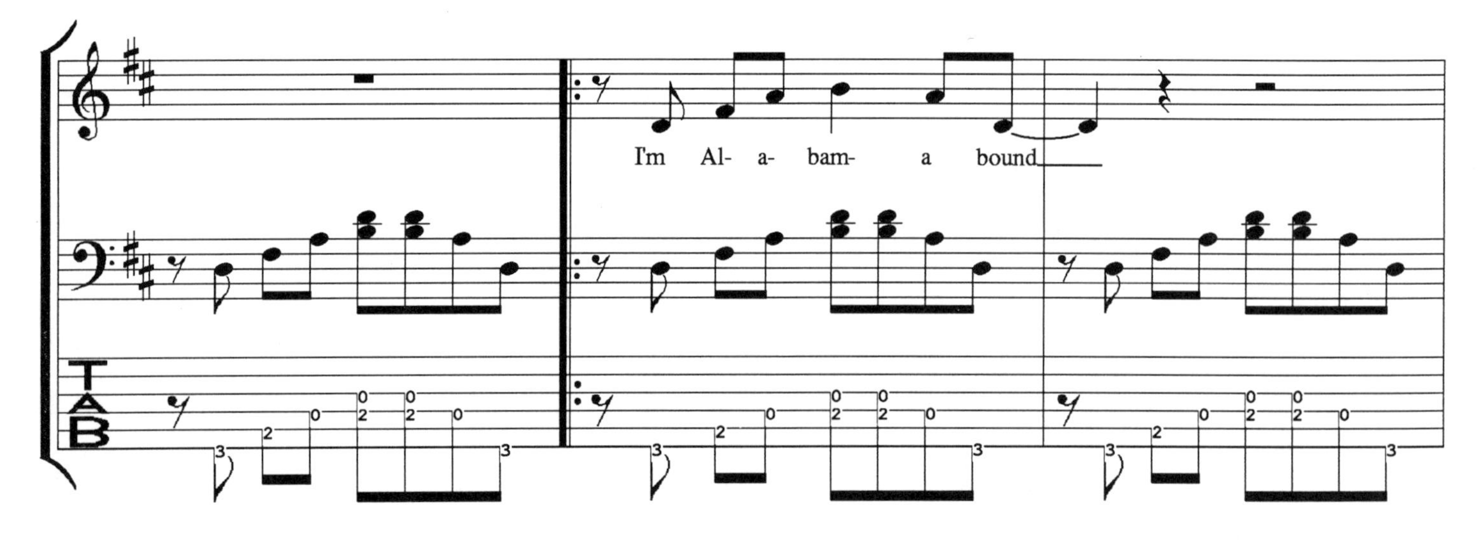

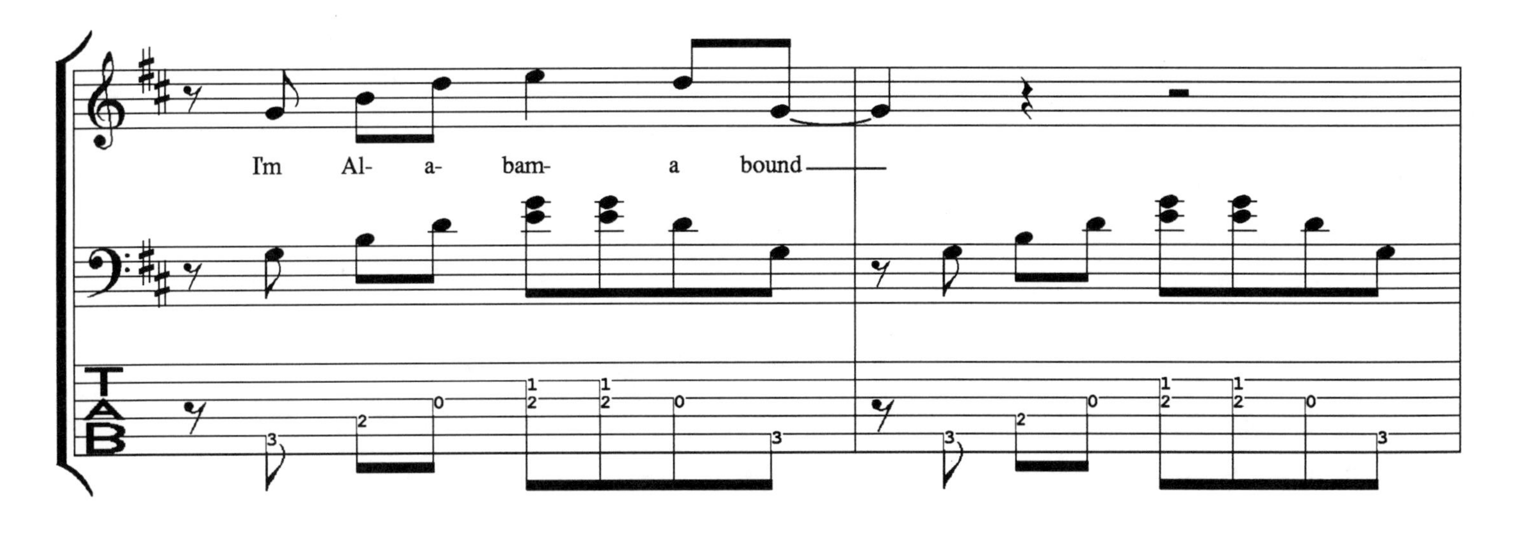
I'm Al- a- bam- a bound

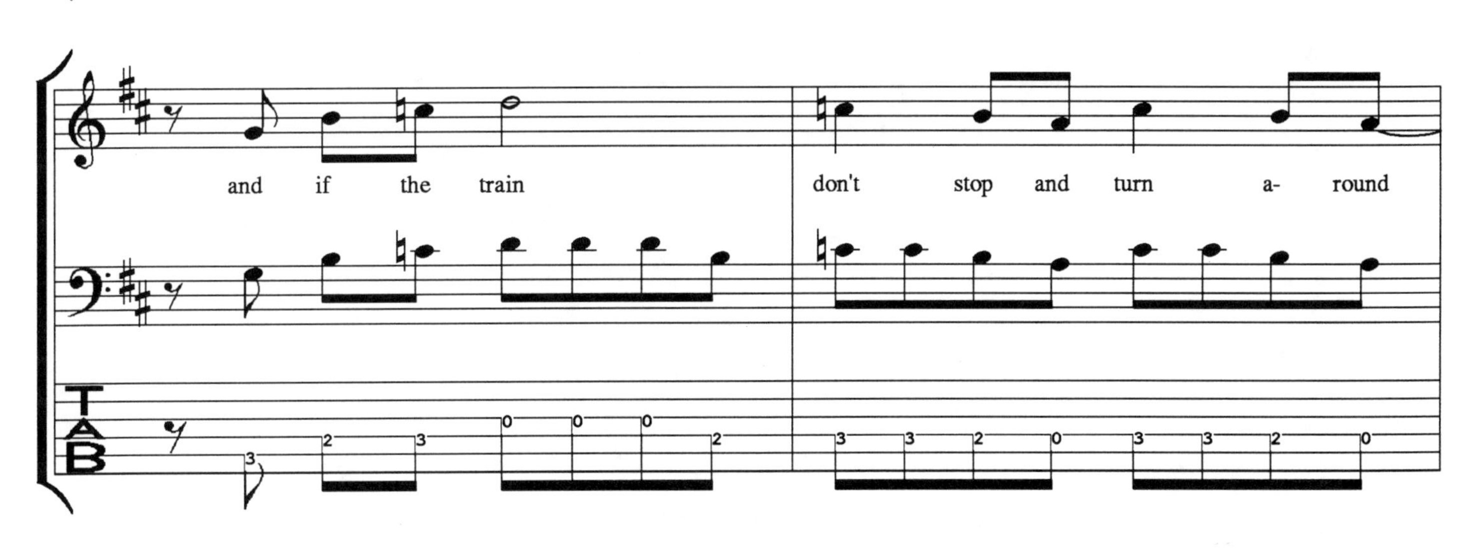
and if the train don't stop and turn a- round

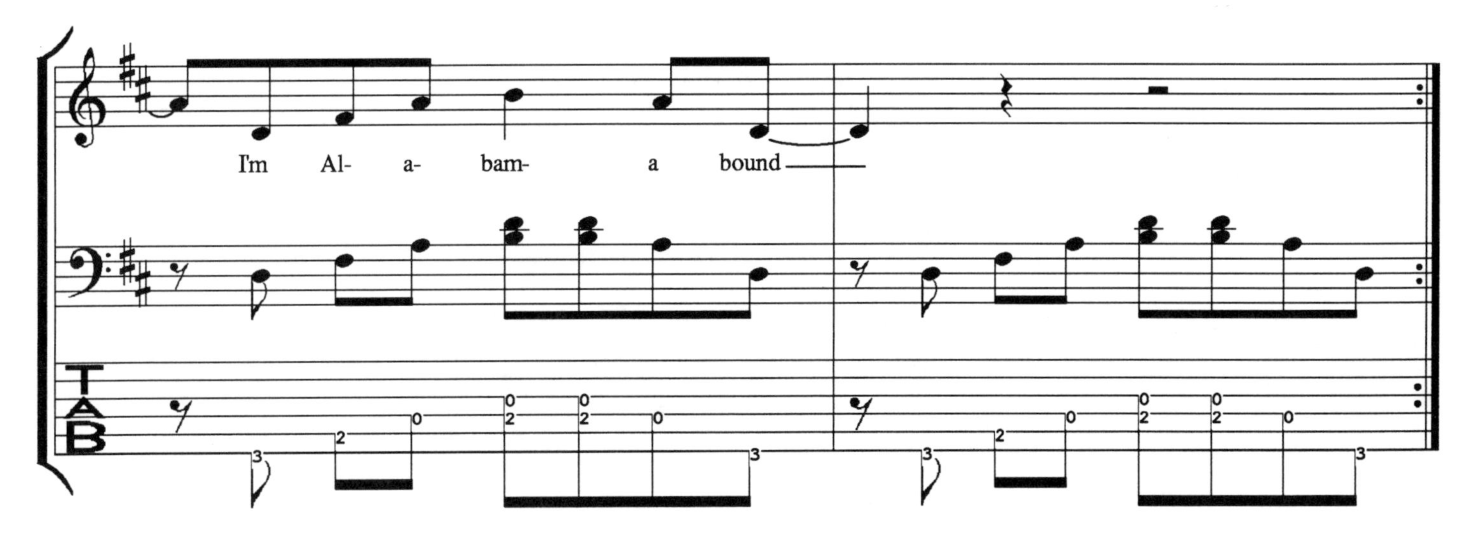
I'm Al- a- bam- a bound

Martha & Huddie (2) Somewhere at Sea
Dec 13, 1943

We have been awful lucky in some ways. We have been able to meet thousands of the very best kind of friends and they have always made their home our home, all because they liked the songs we sang and because you people are so nice. We've had some hard knocks and some rough going, but no matter how hard and rocky the road, our friends never quit us, never let us down, and they're the kind of people that will stick with us always. I know you already know this, but I just want you to know how you made me feel tonight when I heard you on the radio. (Of course Martha knows that what I say goes for her, too, because she is really what makes Leadbelly keep going.) It is now that we're apart that I really see how close we are together. Your guitar and mine both talk the same language - the language of the working people. When our guitars come in there together they talk their own language. I just wish I could have played my guitar along with you tonight, but I couldn't get to it. You can just imagine how I sweated and shook all over, hearing you play, and not able to play with you. The last time we played together was up at Pete & Toshi's wedding party - we had 3 banjos - boy - we really raised the roof that night, didn't we? I want to say I am speaking for our whole crew here on the ship - we all enjoyed your program. How much, I don't guess I could ever write it down.

Well, just remember, we're out here listening to you and thinking about you. Here's to a couple of the nicest folks I ever hope to know -

Your friend as Ever
Woody Guthrie

Letter to Lead Belly and his wife Martha from Woody Guthrie

Bring Me Little Water, Silvy

Transcribed from January 1943 sessions originally released on the Disc series of 78s called "Negro Folk Songs" and now available on *Lead Belly/Where Did You Sleep Last Night?*, Smithsonian Folkways CD 40044, *Lead Belly/In the Shadow of the Gallows Pole*, Tradition CD 1018 and *Lead Belly/Bourgeois Blues*, Collectables CD 5183. Other recordings: 1935 Library of Congress sessions *Lead Belly/Nobody Knows the Trouble I've Seen*, Rounder CD 1098; 1941 WNYC radio broadcast with Anne Graham vocal duet *Folkways: The Original Vision*, Smithsonian Folkways CD 40001; *Lead Belly's Last Sessions*, (1948) with Martha Ledbetter vocal duet, Smithsonian Folkways boxed CD set 40068/71.

July and August is hot and this man's wife – he call her Silvy – and the only way he gets his cool water, he's got to call Silvy to get his water down there 'cause he's burning up. Huddie Ledbetter

Lead Belly narrates this story between sung choruses on the Library of Congress recording. Silvy was his Uncle Bob's wife.

Recent recordings by other musicians include Sweet Honey In The Rock, Pete Seeger and Arlo Guthrie. The Weavers' version "Sylvie", also recorded by Harry Belafonte, was a pop hit in the mid-'50s.

Bring me little water, Silvy,
Bring me little water now.
Bring me little water, Silvy,
Every little once in awhile —
I mean it — every little once in awhile.

Don't you hear me calling?
Don't you hear me now?
Don't you hear me calling
Every little once in awhile?

Don't you see me coming?
Don't you see me now?
Don't you see me coming
Every little once in awhile —
I mean it — every little once in awhile?

You better bring me little water, Silvy,
Bring me little water now.
Bring me little water, Silvy,
Every little once in awhile —
I mean it — every little once in awhile.

(Extra verses from other recordings)

Bring me the bucket, Silvy...

When I hear you callin'...

See me come a-runnin'...

Bring Me Little Water, Silvy

Huddie Ledbetter

edited by John A. Lomax and Alan Lomax

Tempo: 89-105

Tuning: B, E, A, D, F#, B

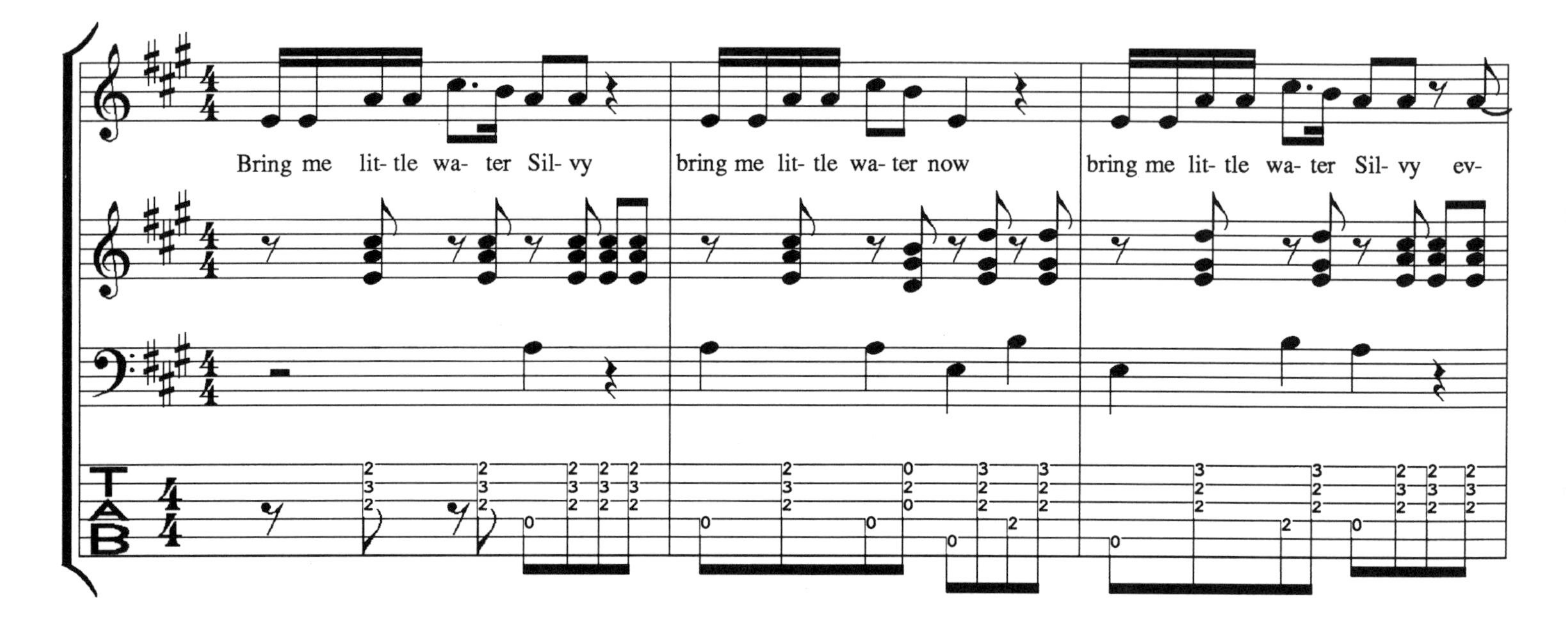

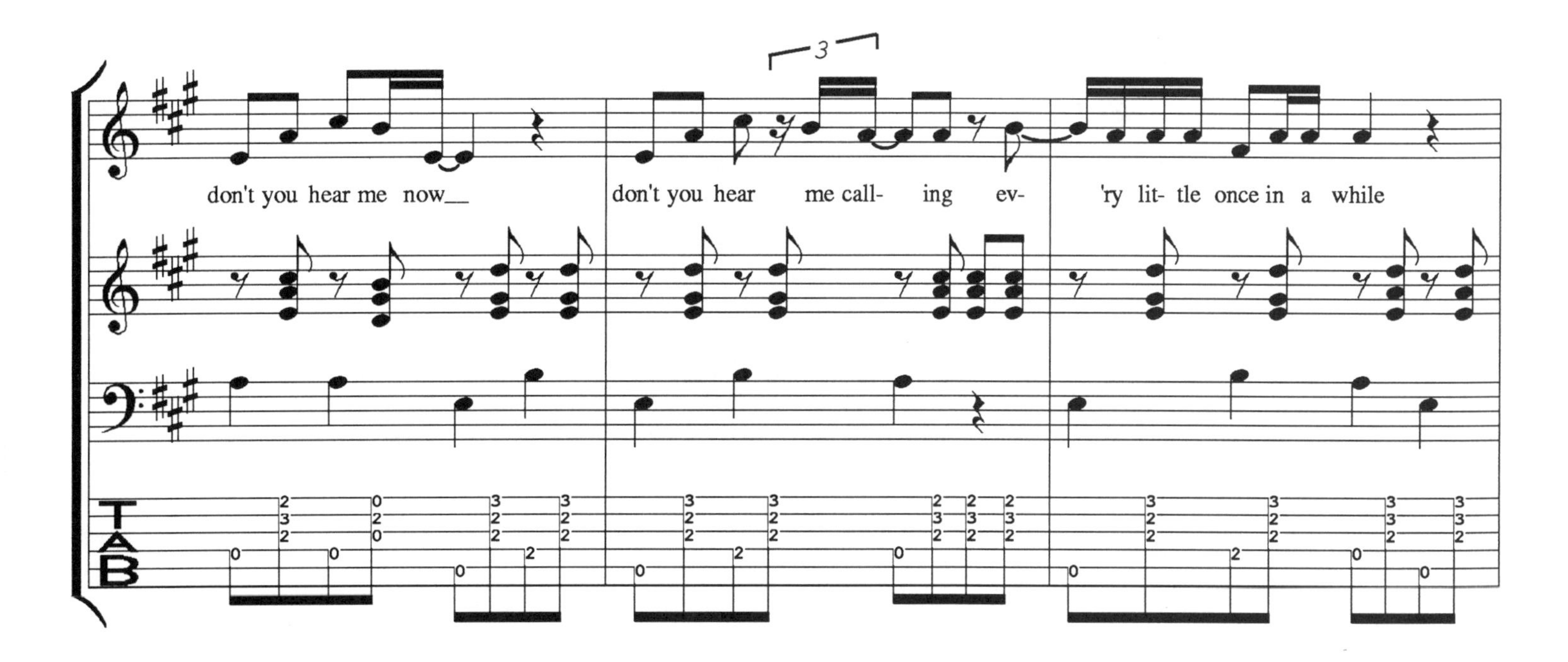
don't you hear me now
don't you hear me call- ing ev-
'ry lit- tle once in a while

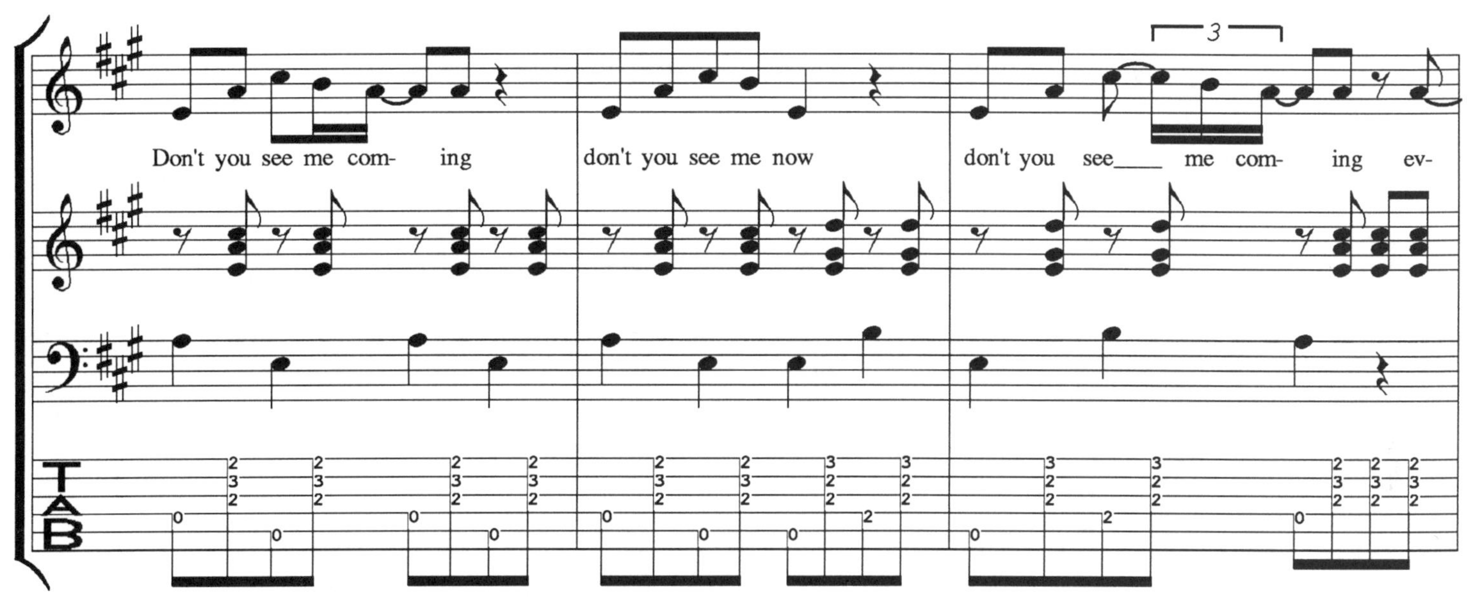
Don't you see me com- ing
don't you see me now
don't you see me com- ing ev-
D.C. al Fine

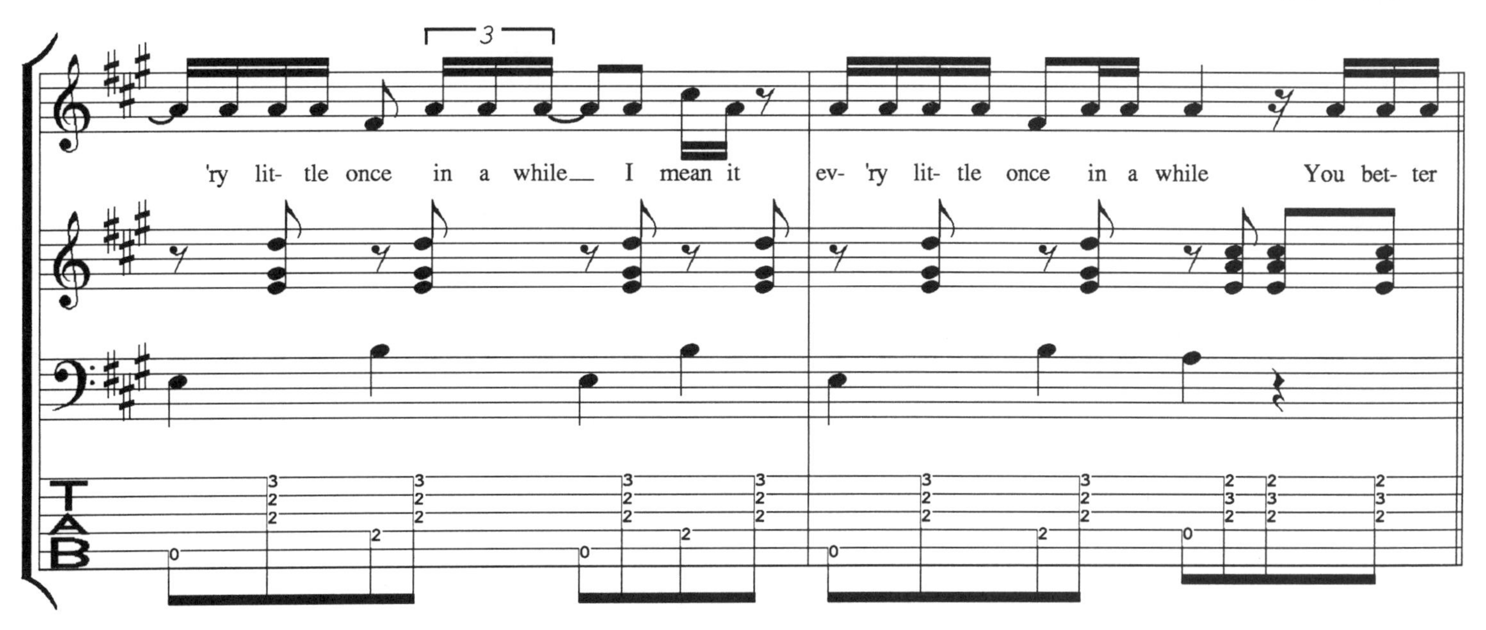
'ry lit- tle once in a while I mean it
ev- 'ry lit- tle once in a while You bet- ter

Christmas Is Coming

(Almost Day) (Chickens Crowin' For Midnight) (Santa Claus Is Coming)

Transcribed from a Feb. 15, 1945 performance in San Francisco now available on *Lead Belly/Where Did You Sleep Last Night?*, Smithsonian Folkways CD 40044. Other Lead Belly CDs: *Leadbelly/Party Songs & Sings and Plays* ("Almost Day" 1944, "Christmas Song" 1941 Asch recordings), Collectables 5609, *Leadbelly* (1944), Capital LP 1821 [on this track Lead Belly is assisted by zitherist Paul Mason Howard; also included on *Christmas Kisses*, compilation Capitol CD CDP 7 94701 2].

Now this is a children's play song when Santa Claus is coming. This is Christmas night. They stay up all day and at midnight they get out in the yard and play. They make the ring and the rooster be crowin'. At midnight he always goin' crow on Christmas night at midnight, and they heard their mama and papa tell 'em that Santa Claus comin'. They ain't gonna go to sleep. Now they gonna get out in the yard and play and sing while they hear that chicken crowin' for midnight. Huddie Ledbetter, 1941

(Chorus)
Christmas is a-comin' and it's a-jumpin'. (3)
Boy it won't be long.

(Verses)
Chicken crows at midnight on a Christmas day.
Rooster crows at midnight on a Christmas day.

Children get so happy on a Christmas day. (2)

(Chorus)
Santa Claus a-comin' and he's a-comin'. (3)
Boy it won't be long.

(Verses)
Santa Claus comes on Christmas, on a Christmas day. (2)

Children run and tell their pappy on a Christmas day. (2)

Little children get so happy on a Christmas day. (2)

("Christmas Song" Collectables recording)
Chicken crowin' for midnight and it's almost day. (4)
Think I heard my mother say it's almost day. (2)
Chicken crowin' for midnight and it's almost day. (4)
Santa Claus is comin', yes, and it's almost day. (2)
Chicken crowin' for midnight and it's Christmas day. (2)
Chicken crowin' for midnight and it's almost day. (4)
Chicken crowin' for midnight and I'm goin' away. (2)
Chicken crowin' for midnight and it's Christmas day. (2)
Chicken crowin' for midnight and it's almost day. (2)
Think I heard my papa say it's almost day. (2)
Chicken crowin' for midnight and it's almost day. (2)
Christmas is a-comin' and it's almost day. (2)
Childrens all is happy and it's almost day.
Childrens all is happy on a Christmas day.

(additional verses from Capitol recording)
Old Santa Claus movin' in on a Christmas day.
Children all get so happy on a Christmas day.
Children get out in the yard and swing on Christmas day.
Everybody gets happy on a Christmas day.
Children is a-walkin' on a Christmas day.
All children is a-talkin' on Christmas day.

Christmas Is Coming

(Almost Day) (Chickens Crowin' For Midnight) (Santa Claus Is Coming)

Huddie Ledbetter

Tempo: 98-105

Tuning: B, E, A, D, F#, B

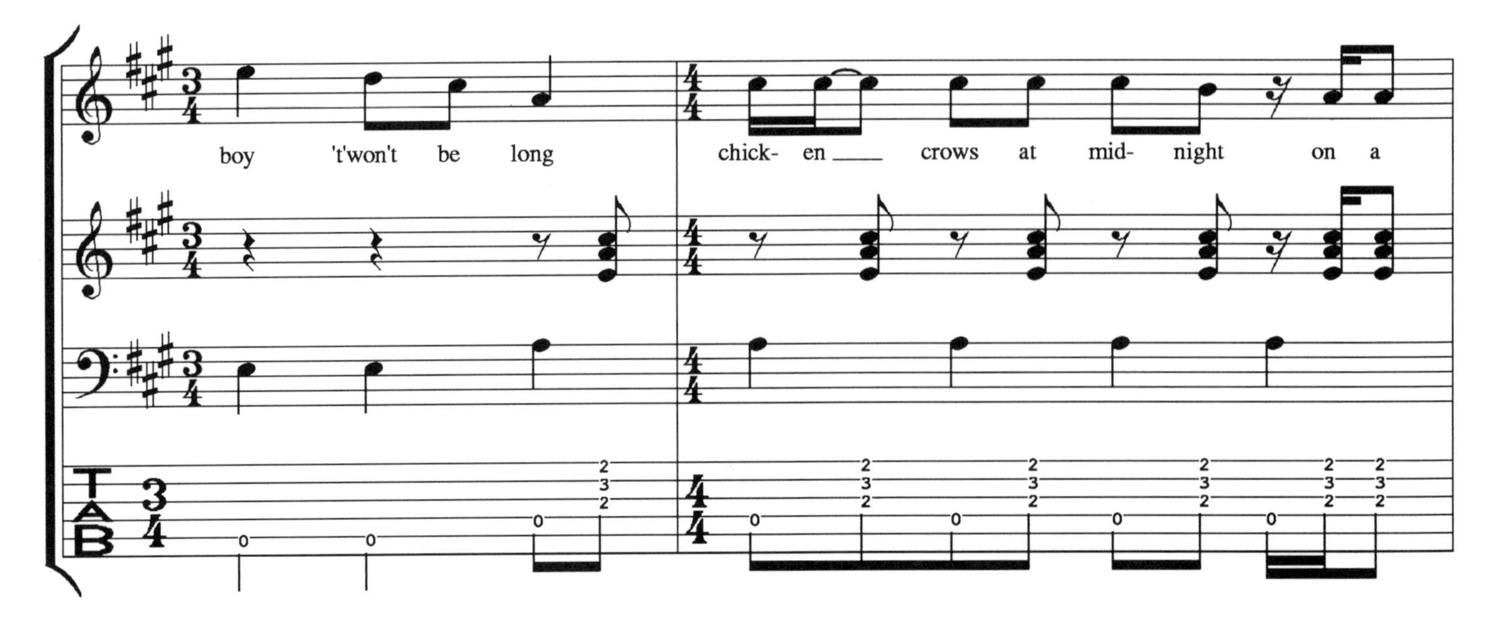
boy 't'won't be long
chick- en crows at mid- night on a
T
A
B

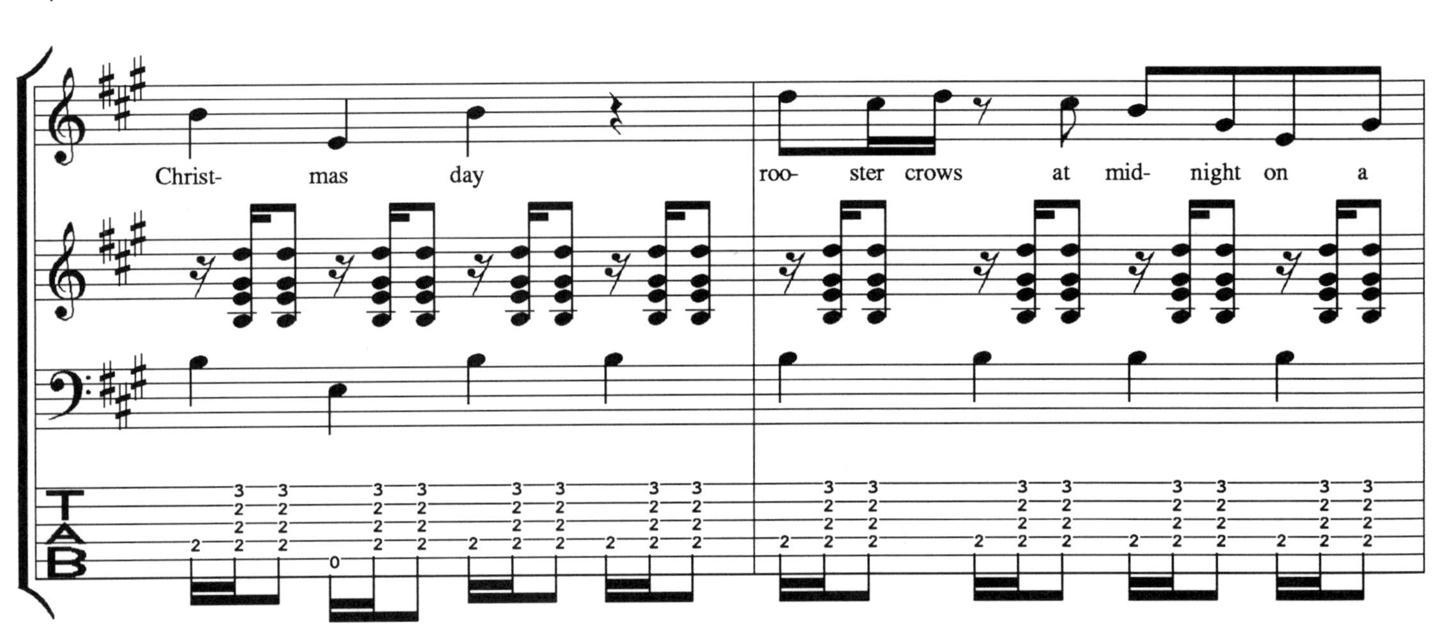
Christ- mas day
roo- ster crows at mid- night on a
T
A
B

Christ- mas day
child- ren get so hap- py on a
T
A
B

Thursday Evening, Oct. 11

8:15 P. M.

Roosevelt Junior High School

3366 Park Boulevard

The Women's Civic League

PRESENT

"Lead Belly"

INTERNATIONALLY ACCLAIMED ONE OF AMERICA'S GREATEST FOLK BALLADIST

—and—

ONLY MUSICIAN IN THE WORLD WHO PLAYS THE 12-STRING GUITAR

Born of American Negro parents, he sings singful songs, religious songs, work ballads

—and—

TALKING BLUES

HIS MUSIC INSPIRES CHILDREN AND DELIGHTFULLY KEEPS HIS AUDIENCE SWAYED TO HUMAN EMOTIONS. UNDISPUTABLE HIS IS SOMETHING DIFFERENT IN MUSICAL ENTERTAINMENT

ADMISSION..*$1.81*

TICKETS ON SALE AT THEARLE'S MUSIC CO.
HELEN LYTER AT THE BOX OFFICE

Program cover from 1945 performance in San Diego Lead Belly Archives

Lining Track

(Can't You Line 'Em) (Line 'Em)

Transcribed from 1944 Asch sessions available on *Leadbelly Sings Folk Songs* and *Lead Belly/Bourgeois Blues*, Smithsonian Folkways CDs 40010 and 40045. Other CD recordings: *Lead Belly/In the Shadow of the Gallows Pole* (first issued in a 1943 78rpm album *Negro Folk Songs as Sung by Leadbelly*), Tradition 1018; *Leadbelly/Alabama Bound* (1940 RCA sessions with the Golden Gate Quartet), RCA 9600-2-R. The rock group Aerosmith interpolated part of the song into their "Hangman's Jury." John Denver recorded it on his CD entitled *All Aboard.*

This is a track lining chant sung in unison while aligning the rails on a railroad track. The workmen, sometimes called "gandy dancers", would sing and move the track in time with the response line. Ella Louise was a woman who headed a track crew.

Oh boys, is you right, done got right.
All I hate about lining track, these old bars about to break my back, ah.

Chorus:
Ho boys, can't you line 'em? (shack a lack a) (3)
See Ella Louise go lining track.

Moses stood on the Red Sea shore
Smoting that water with a two-by-four. (Chorus)

If I could I surely would
Stand on the rock where Moses stood. (Chorus)

Mary and the baby lyin' in the shade
Thinkin' 'bout the money that I ain't made. (Chorus)

(additional verses from RCA recording)
All I want is two lie two,
*You gotta join that 802.**

If you want to sing on the radio,
*You gotta join that APARO.**

I went down on a two cent track
Begging my baby to take me back.

I went down that TP line
Begging that woman won't she be mine.

*reference to local unions

Lining Track

(Can't You Line 'Em) (Line 'Em)

Huddie Ledbetter

Tempo: 87, accent on beat and counter beat

A Cappella

Keep Your Hands Off Her

Transcribed from 1944 Asch sessions with Woody Guthrie, Cisco Houston and Sonny Terry available on *Leadbelly Sings Folk Songs*, Smithsonian Folkways CD 40010 and *Leadbelly/Defense Blues*, Collectables CD 5196.

Keep your hands off her – keep your hands off her. (2)
Keep your hands off her – you hear what I say.
You know she don't belong to you.

She's a heavy-hipted mama - she's got some great big legs. (3)
Walking like she's walking on soft-boiled eggs. (Chorus)

Her name is Josey and she ain't so nosy. (3)
But boy, she sure cosy. (*Chorus*)

She's a heavy-hipted mama and she's built up straight. (3)
She's got just what it takes. (*Chorus*)

Lead Belly and Josh White Lead Belly Archives

Keep Your Hands Off Her

Huddie Ledbetter

Tempo: 125-135

Tuning: B, E, A, D, F#, B

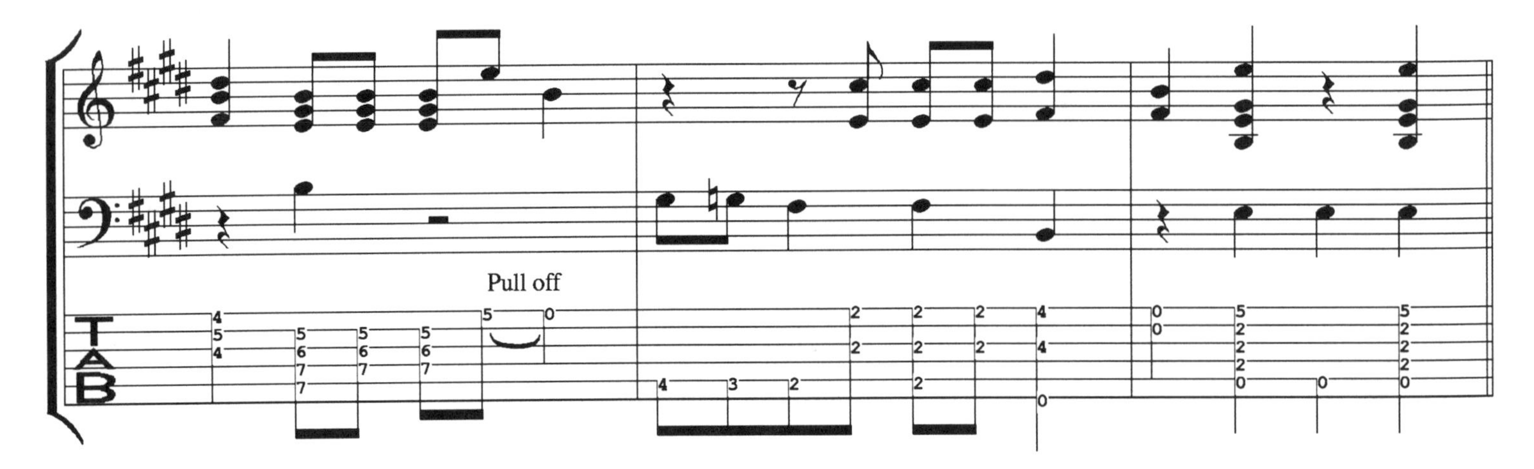
Pull off

Keep your hands off her
keep your hands off her

Keep your hands off her

keep your hands off her
Keep your hands off her

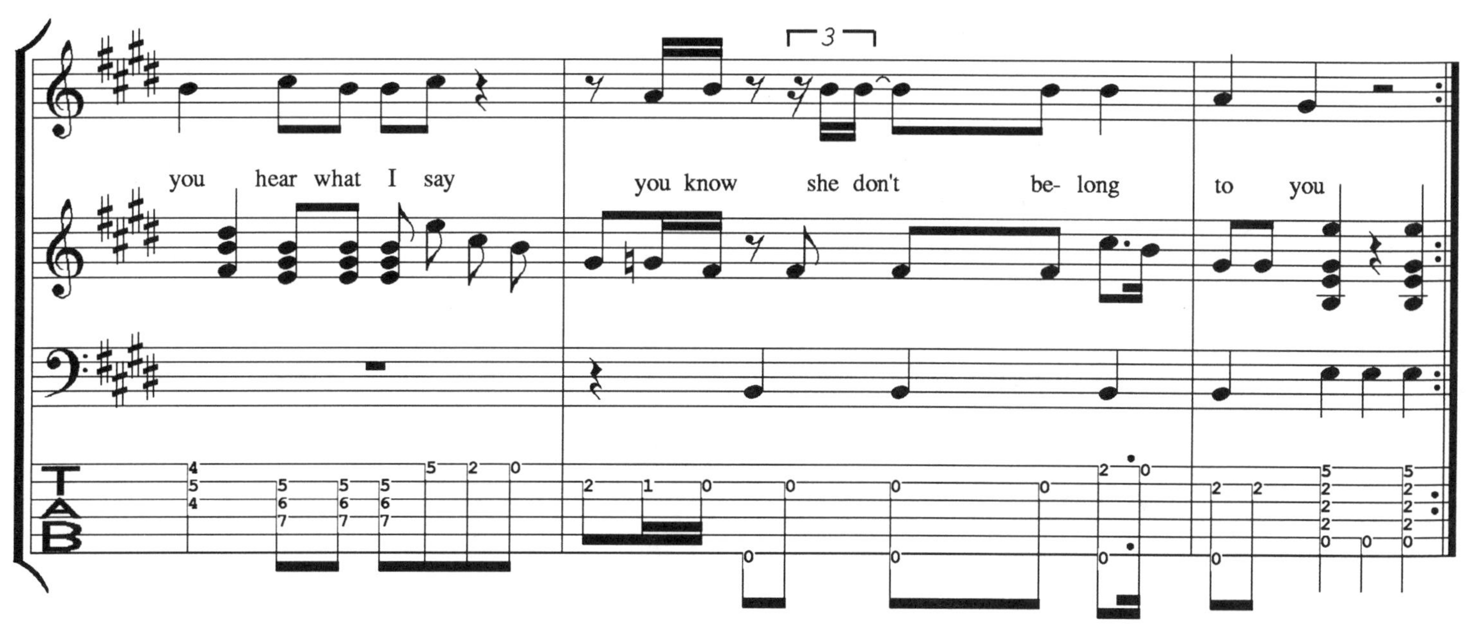
you hear what I say
you know she don't be- long to you
3

Midnight Special

Transcribed from *Lead Belly's Last Sessions* (1948), Smithsonian Folkways boxed CD set 40068/71.
Other CD recordings: *Lead Belly/Midnight Special* (1934 Angola Prison recording by the Lomaxes for the Library of Congress), Rounder 1044; *Folkways: The Original Vision*, Smithsonian Folkways 40001, *Leadbelly/Defense Blues* and *Leadbelly Party Songs/Sings & Plays*, Collectables 4196 and 5609 (recorded in 1946 for Disc Records); *Leadbelly/Alabama Bound* (1940 RCA sessions with the Golden Gate Quartet), RCA 9600-2-R; *Lead Belly/Bourgeois Blues* (undated and previously unreleased), Smithsonian Folkways 40045.

The Weavers' 1952 recording was a pop hit and the song has become a folk standard in the repertoires of artists such as Arlo Guthrie and Pete Seeger.

The title refers to a train which ran by Sugarland Prison at night and came to symbolize freedom.

"Yonder comes Miss Rosie."
"How in the world do you know?"
"Well, I know her by the apron
And the dress she wore.
Umbrella on her shoulder,
A piece of paper in her hand,
Well, I'm gonna ask the captain
To turn a-loose of my man."

Chorus:
Let the Midnight Special
Shine its light on me.
Let the Midnight Special
Shine its ever-lovin' light on me.

PROCLAMATION
BY THE
Governor of the State of Texas

TO ALL TO WHOM THESE PRESENTS SHALL COME:

WHEREAS, At the May Term, A. D., 1918, of the District Court of [illegible] County, Texas, [illegible]
WALTER BOYD
was convicted of a felony, to-wit; Assault to murder, and his punishment assessed at thirty five (35) years confinement in the State Penitentiary; and

WHEREAS, applicant has now served a part of his sentence with a clear prison record and executive clemency is granted for the reason that it is believed applicant has been sufficiently punished for the offense committed, and that he will make a good law-abiding citizen after his release.

NOW, THEREFORE, I, PAT M. NEFF, Governor of Texas, do, by virtue of the authority vested in me by the Constitution and laws of the State of Texas, hereby grant the said WALTER BOYD a full pardon, hereby restoring him to full citizenship, giving him the full right to testify in any and all courts, and the full right of suffrage.

IN TESTIMONY WHEREOF, I have hereunto signed my name officially and caused the Seal of State to be hereon impressed, at the City of Austin, Texas, this [illegible] day of January, A. D., 192[illegible].

Governor of Texas

BY THE GOVERNOR:

Secretary of State

Lead Belly's pardon from Texas Governor Pat Neff (Walter Boyd had been Lead Belly's alias) Lead Belly Archives

When you get up in the morning,
When that big bell ring,
Go marching to the table,
You meet the same old thing.
Knife and fork are on the table,
Ain't nothing in my pan;
Ever say anything about it,
Have a trouble with the man. (Chorus)

If you ever go to Houston,
Boy, you better walk right,
And you better not squabble,
And you better not fight.
Bason and Brock will arrest you,*
Payson and Boone will take you down;*
You can bet your bottom dollar
That you're Sugarland bound. (Chorus)

Well, jumpin' little Judy
She was a mighty fine girl,
Well, Judy brought jumpin'
To this whole round world.
Well, she brought it in the morning
Just a while 'fore day,
When she brought me the news
That my wife was dead.

That started me to grievin',
Whoopin', hollerin' and cryin',
Then I began to worry
'Bout my great long time. (Chorus)

(Pete Seeger's tribute verse)
Old Huddie Ledbetter
He was a mighty fine man.
He taught us this song
And to the whole wide land.
But now he's done with all his grieving,
His whoopin', hollerin' and a-cryin'.
Now he's done with all his studyin'
About his great long time.

*Popular song version substitutes "the sheriff" for the various police officers' names and "penitentiary" for "Sugarland."

Midnight Special

Huddie Ledbetter

edited by John A. Lomax and Alan Lomax

Tempo: 160-170

Tuning: B, E, A, D, F#, B

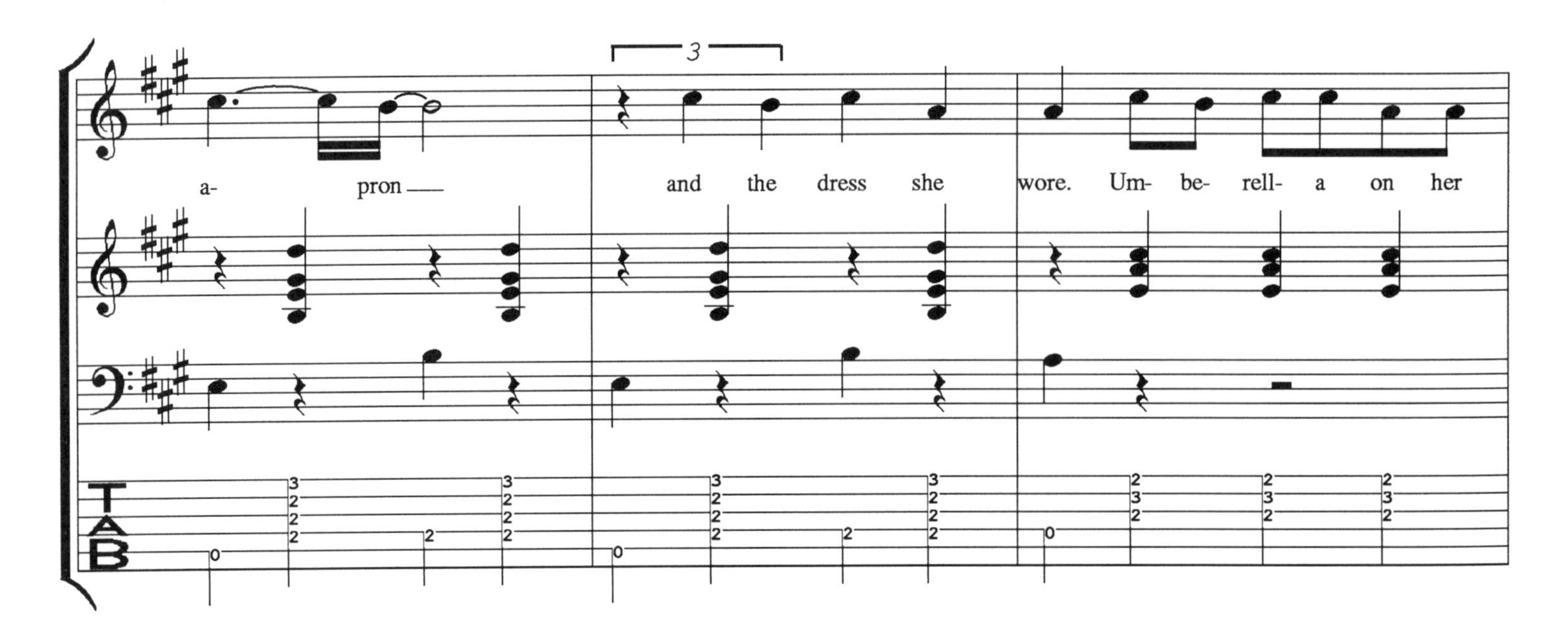
3
a- pron
and the dress she
wore. Um- be- rell- a on her

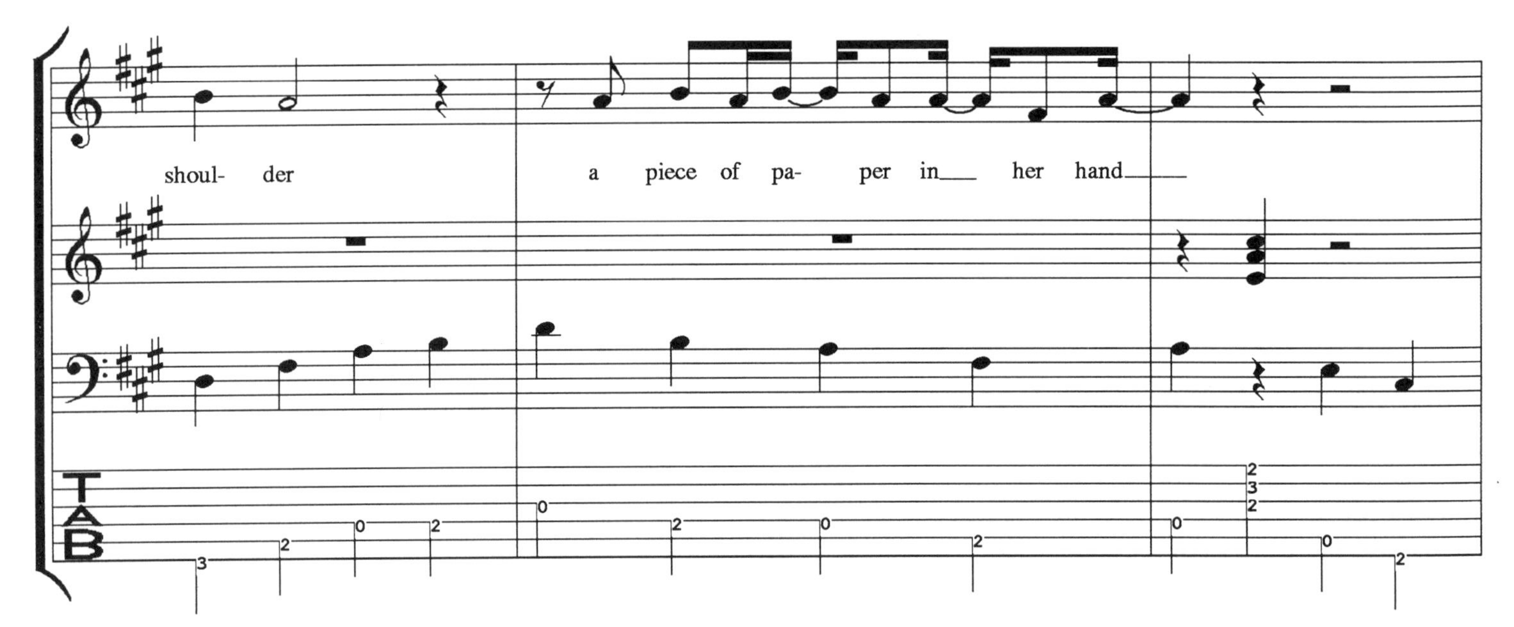
shoul- der
a piece of pa- per in her hand

Well I'm gon- na ask the
cap- tain
to turn a- loose of my man

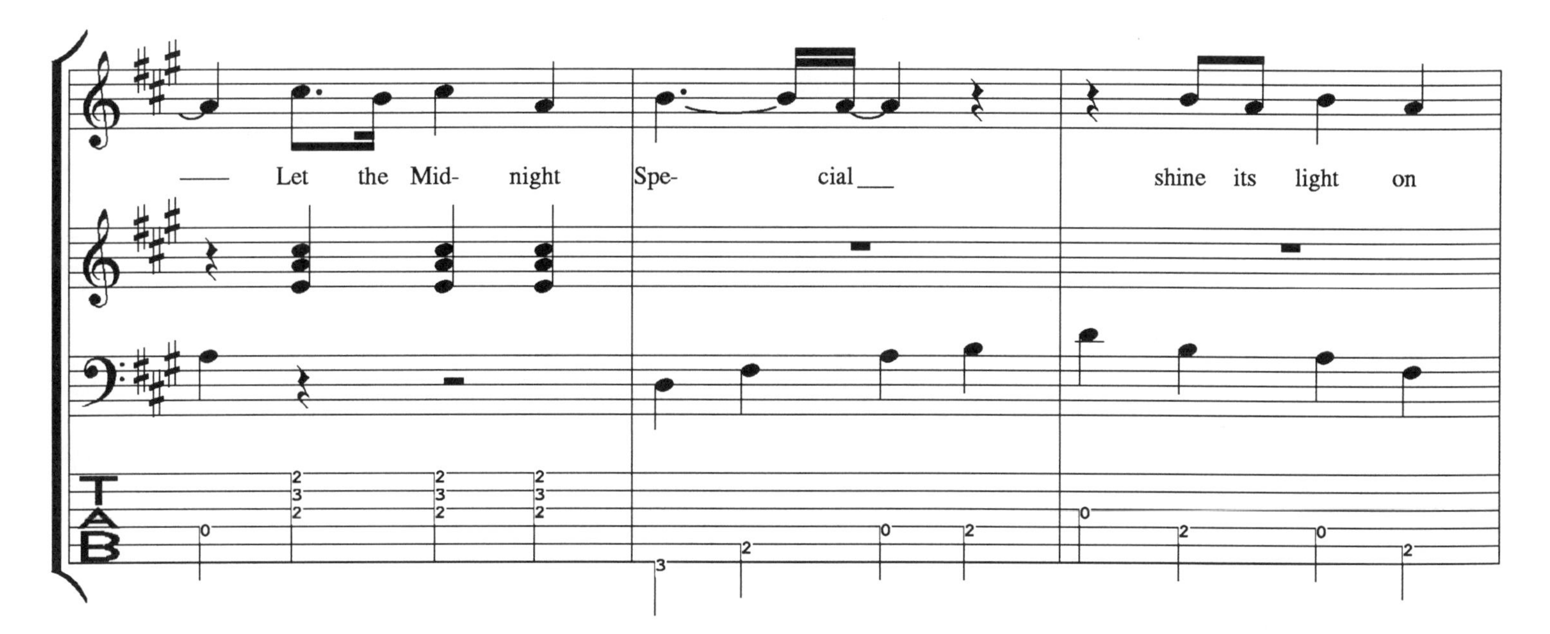
Let the Mid- night Spe- cial
shine its light on

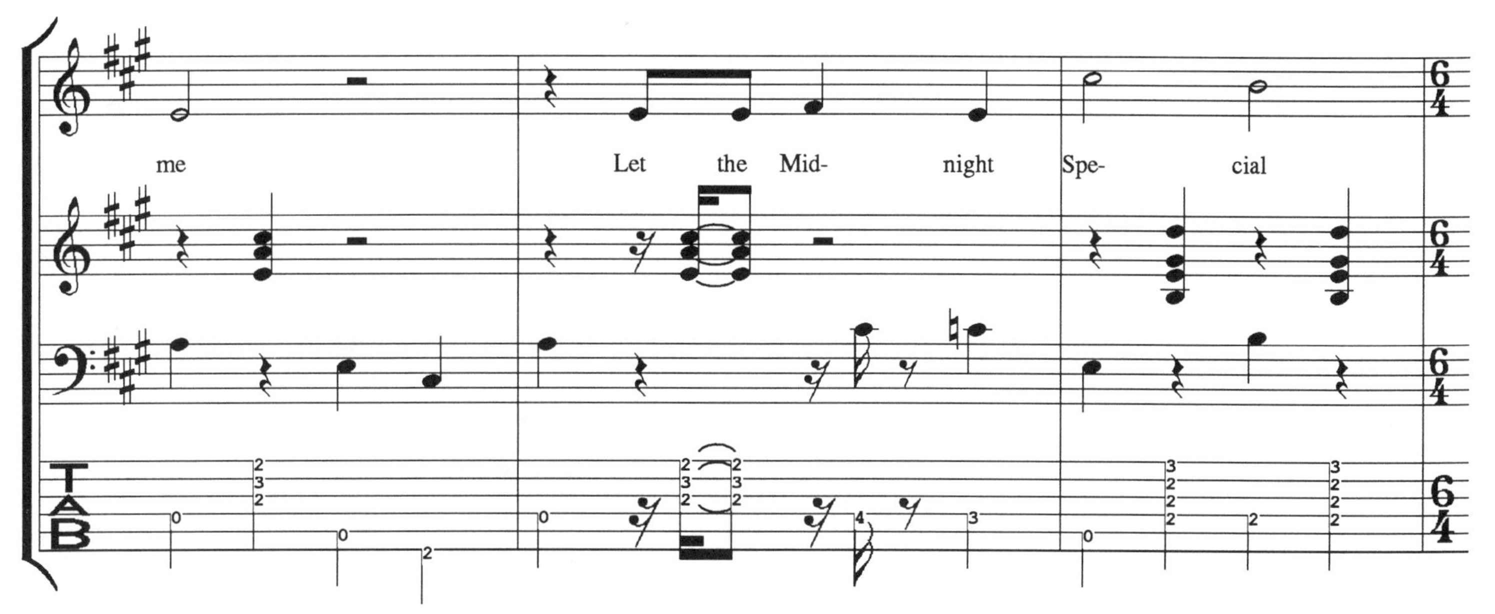
me
Let the Mid- night Spe- cial

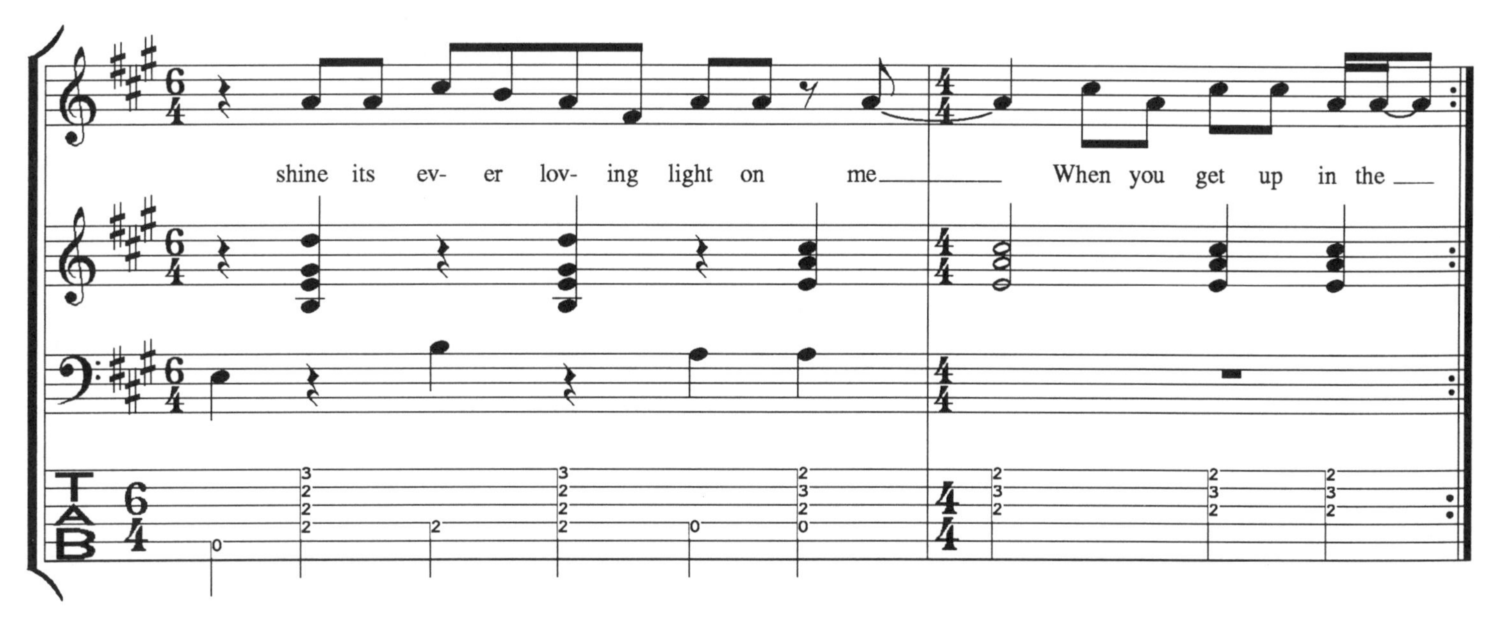
shine its ev- er lov- ing light on me
When you get up in the

4, 5 and 9

Transcribed from the 1948 *Lead Belly's Last Sessions* now available on Smithsonian Folkways CD set 40068/71. An out-take from a 1946 Asch studio session brings together Lead Belly, Sonny Terry, Brownie McGhee, Willie "The Lion" Smith and Pops Foster and has been released on Smithsonian Folkways CD 40044 *Where Did You Sleep Last Night?*

This song reflects some of Lead Belly's disillusionment with the Grade B reception Hollywood accorded him. When Lead Belly asked for a screen test, an executive told him to call him the next morning at 45 to 9. Lead Belly didn't know this was a Sunset Boulevard brush-off. He took the remark literally, put through a call at quarter past eight and was laughed off the switchboard.

I called her this morning between four, five and nine (3)
I want you to meet me on Hollywood and Vine.

If you get there just before I do,
You can tell your friends that I'm coming too.

I'm gonna sing this verse, and I ain't gonna sing it no more.
Next time I sing it, I'm gonna be in Chicago.

Lead Belly Archives

4, 5 and 9

Huddie Ledbetter

Tempo: 130-145

Tuning: C,F,A#,D#,G,C

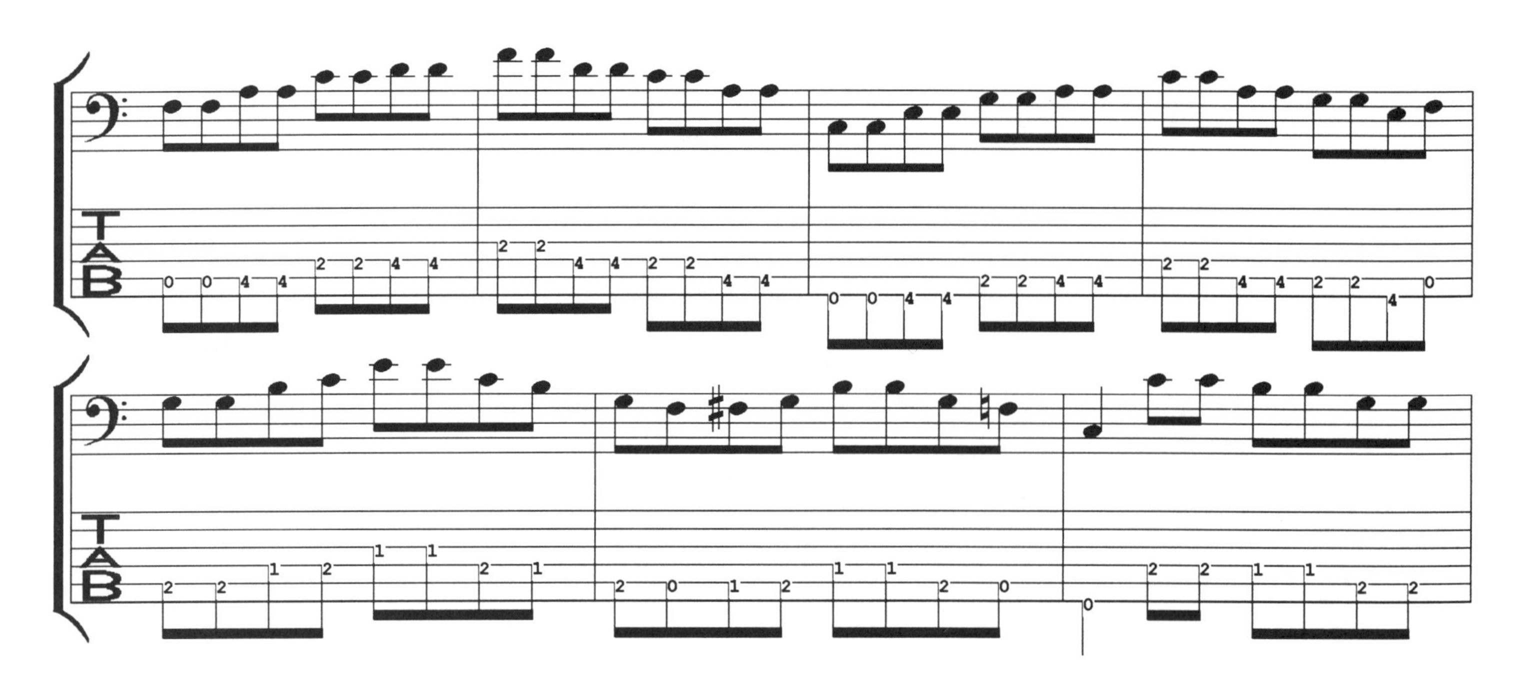

I called her this morn- ing 'tween four five and nine

I called her this morn- ing 'tween four

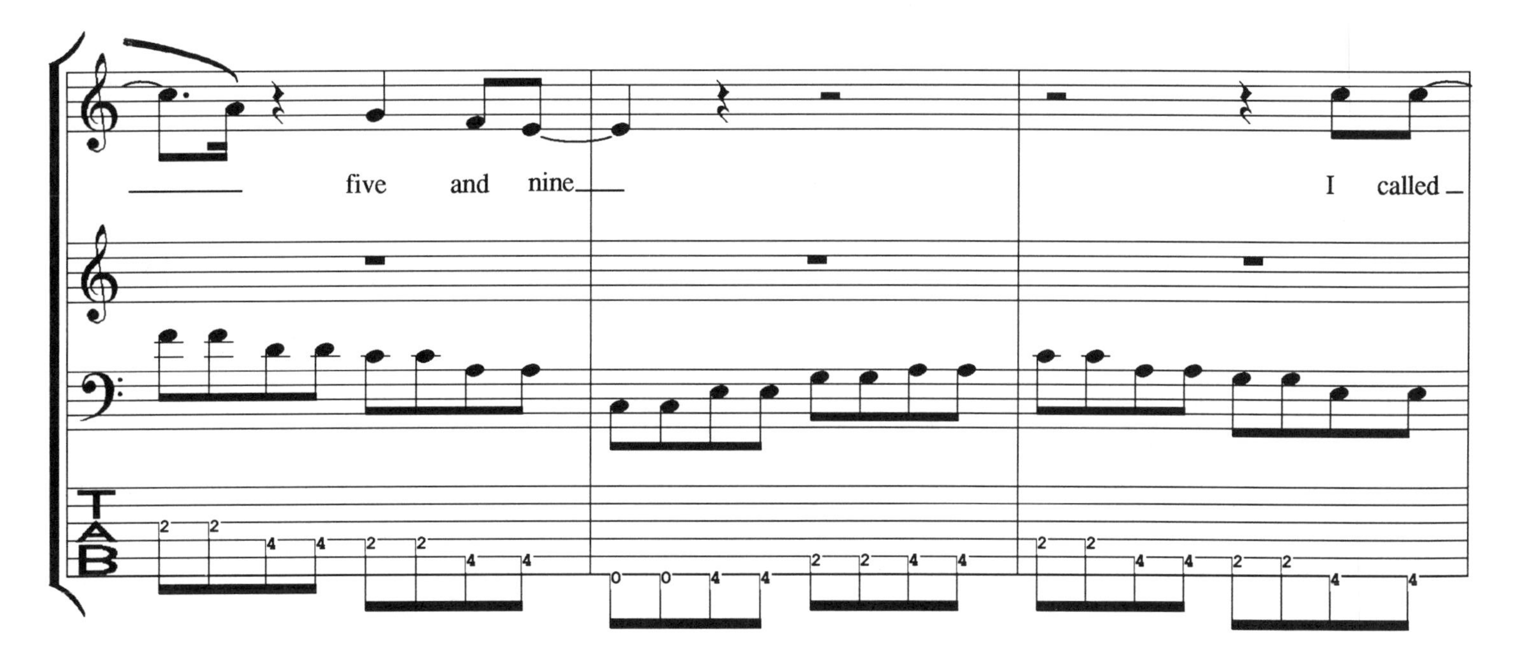
five and nine
I called
TAB

her this morn- ing 'tween
four five and nine
TAB

I
want you to meet me on
Hol-ly- wood and Vine
TAB

If you
get there
just be- fore I do
T
A
B

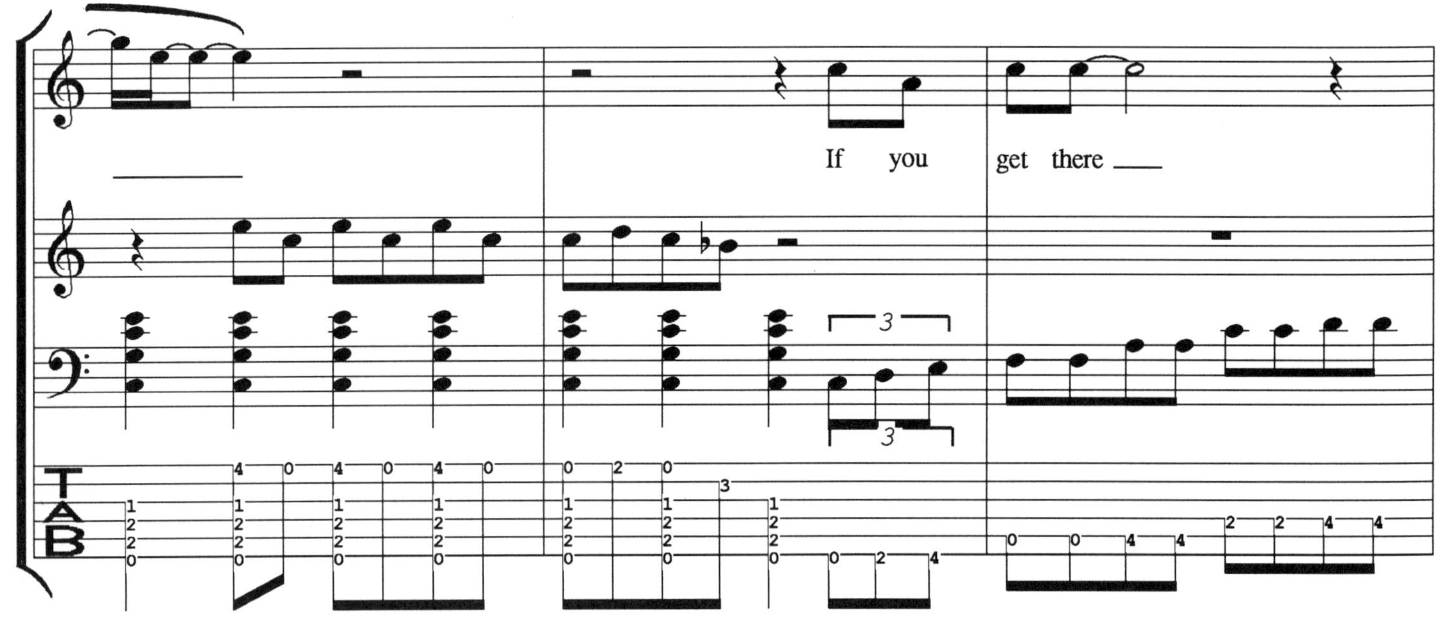
If you
get there
3
3
T
A
B

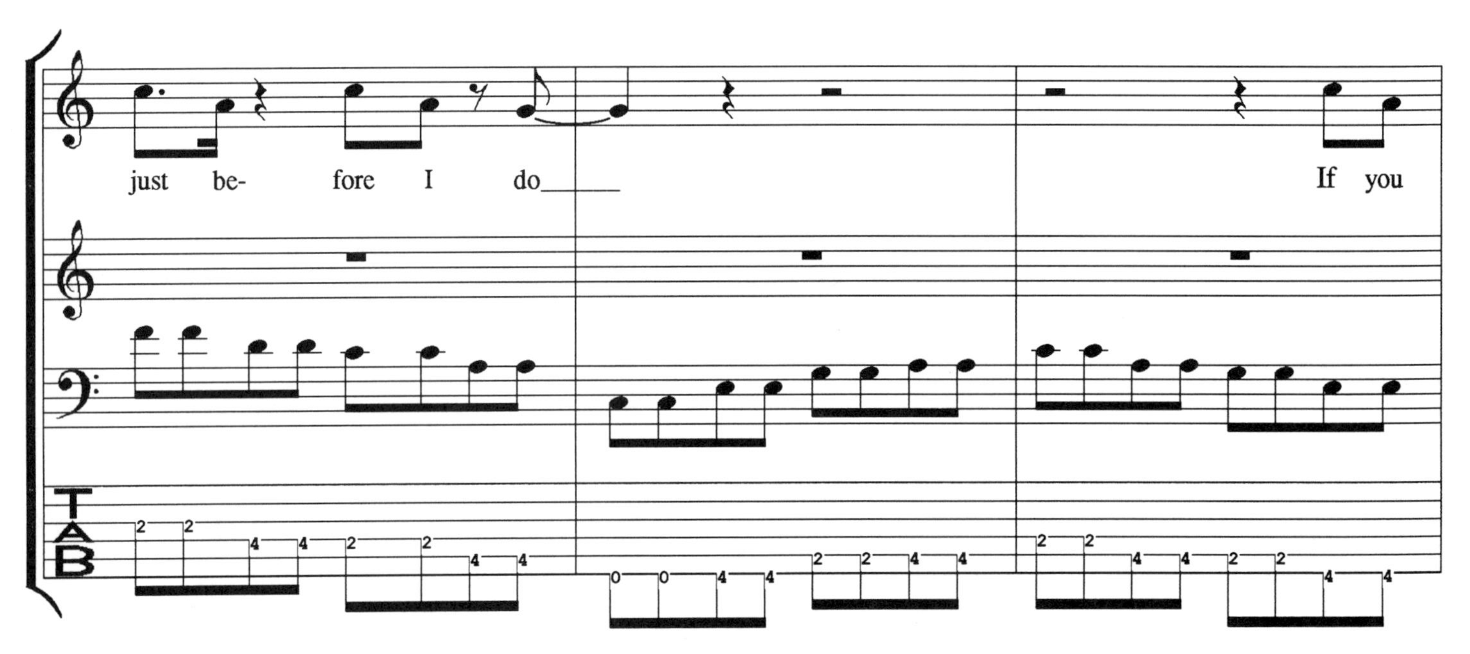
just be- fore I do
If you
T
A
B

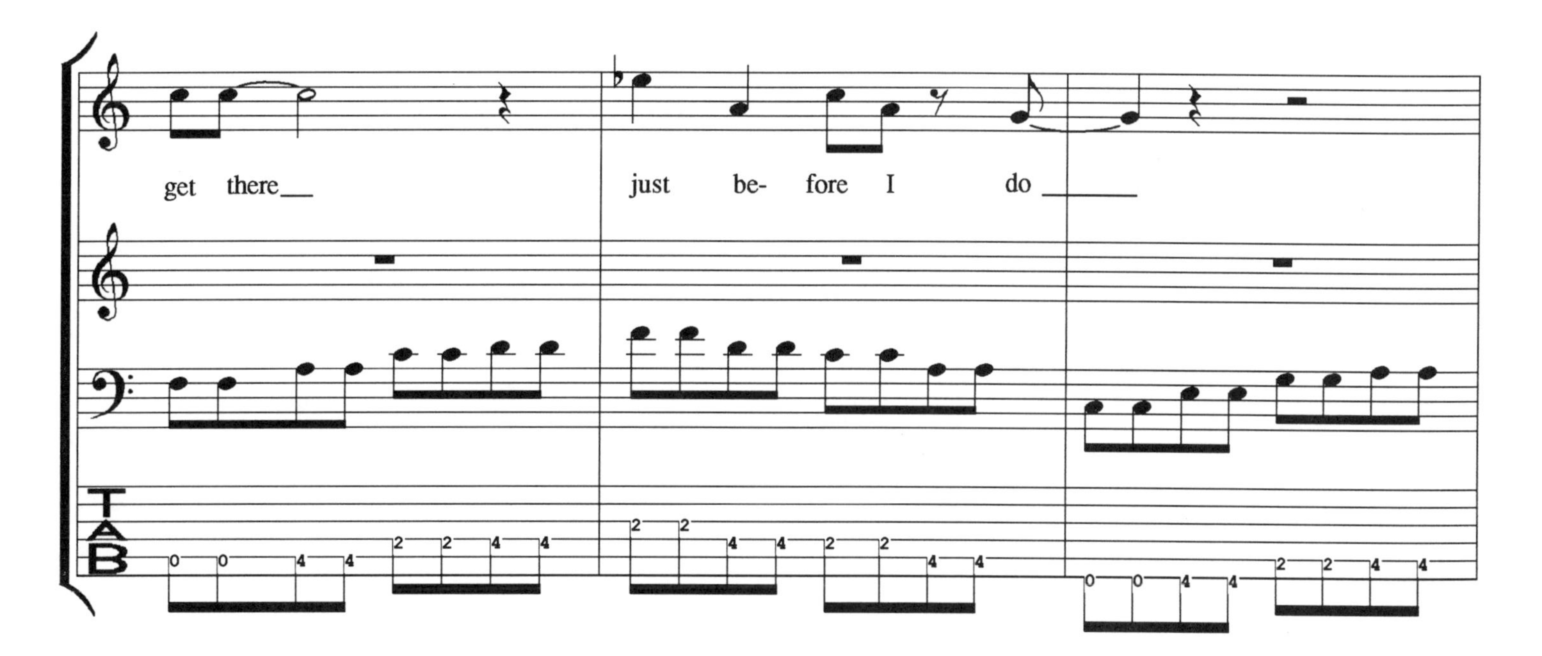
get there
just be- fore I do

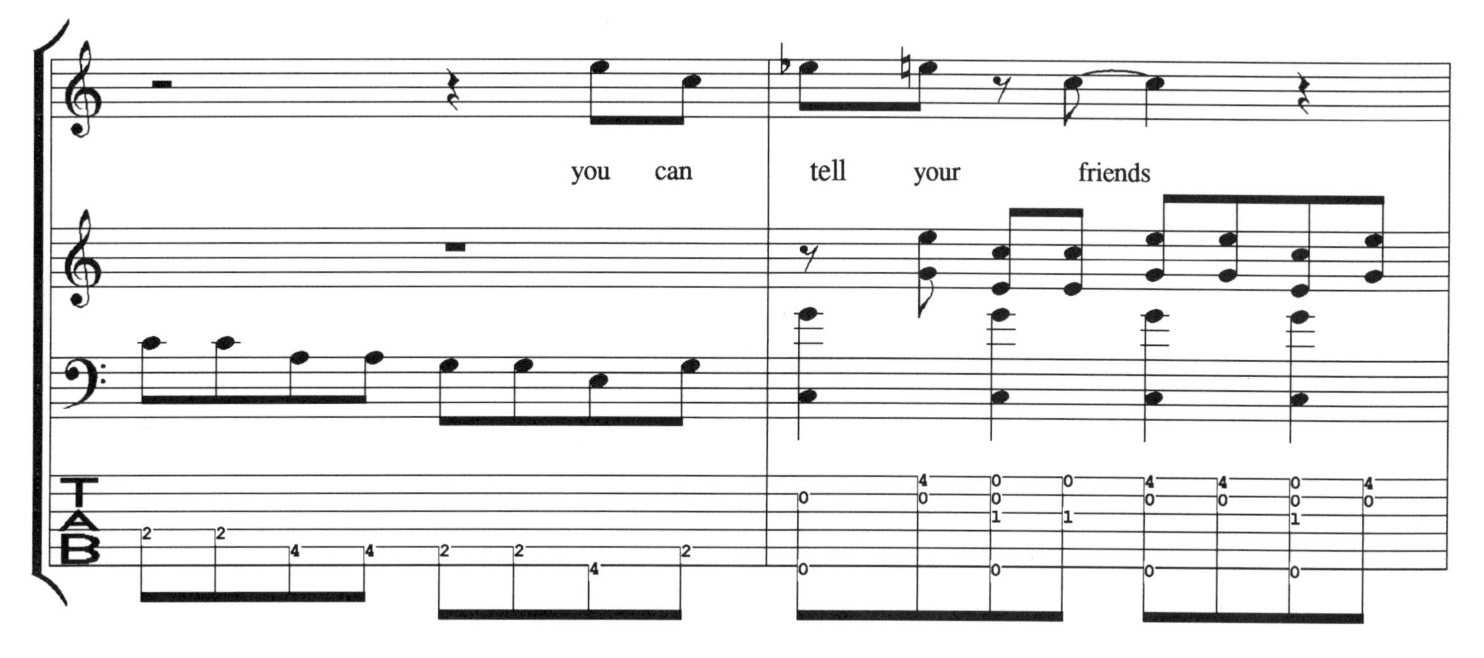
you can tell your friends

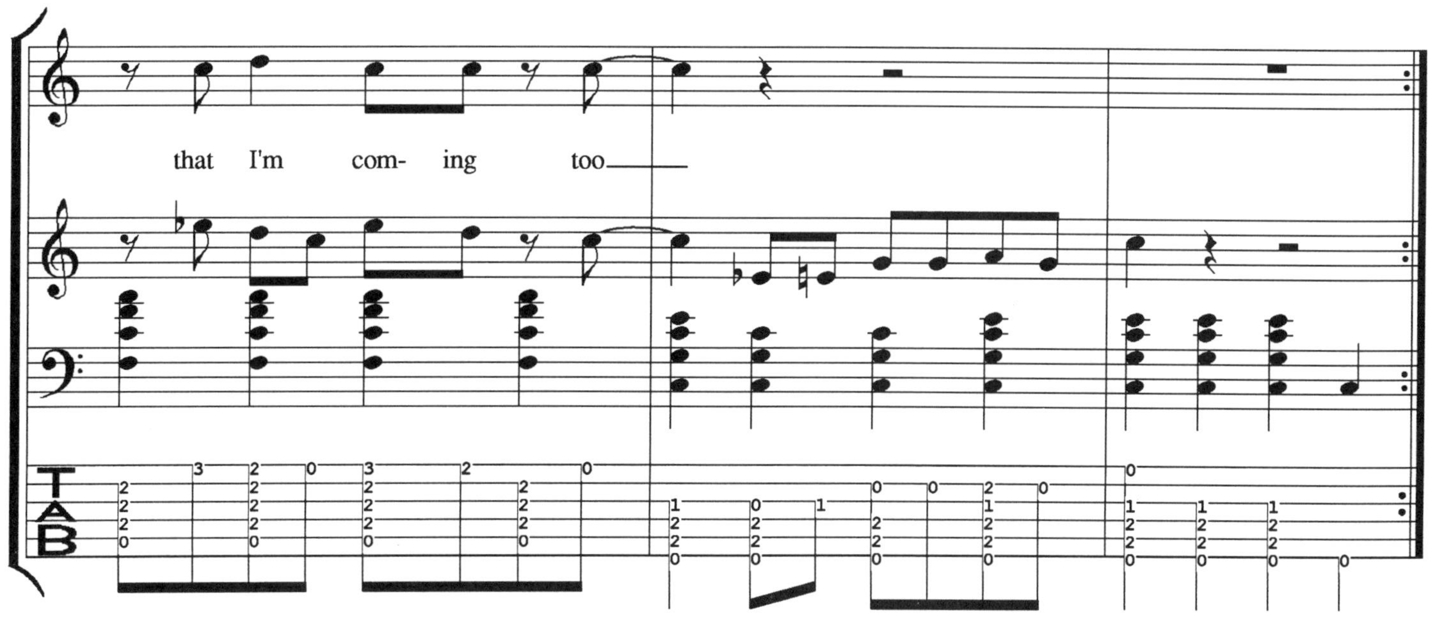
that I'm com- ing too

Roberta

Transcribed from 1939 Musicraft sessions now available on *Lead Belly/Goodnight Irene*, Tradition CD 1006. Other CD recordings: *Leadbelly/King of the 12-String Guitar* and *Leadbelly* (1935 ARC sessions), Columbia CK 46776 and CK 30035; *Lead Belly/Midnight Special* (1935 Library of Congress sessions), Rounder 1044; *Leadbelly/Alabama Bound* (1940 RCA sessions), RCA 9600-2-R

When I used to play down on Fannin Street in Shreveport an' all the women would get about half-drunk, they'd b'gin to holler an' tell me, say, 'Baby, play us Roberta!' I'd sing 'em 'bout Roberta an' they'd all b'gin to cry.

Huddie Ledbetter, 1936

Oh Roberta, tell me how long, how long (2)
You gonna keep me down here, baby, singing this same old song.

I'm down on the river sittin' down on the ground,
I'm going to stay right here till that steamboat come down.

Way up the river just as far as I can see,
I thought I spied my old time used-to-be.

She's a brown-skinned woman and she's got long, black, wavy hair.
That woman looks so good, baby, she can treat me most anywhere.

I'm goin' to the station, talk to that chief o' police.
Tell him that Roberta done quit me, I can't see no peace.

Oh Roberta, don't you hear me callin' you.
I got just one more thing, baby, I want you to do.

(additional verses from Columbia recording)
Oh Roberta, don't know where you been so long.
Yes, I been 'cross the country with my long clothes on.

Oh Roberta, sit down on my knee,
I've got a lot to tell you and that's been worryin' me.

I thought I spied my old time used-to-be,
And it was nothin', honey, but a cypress tree.

Tell me, Roberta, what's the matter with you?
This man ain't got nobody to take his troubles to.

(Rounder recording)
You're a brown-skin woman, chocolate to the bone,
And you know good and well I can't leave you alone.

(RCA recording)
Oh Roberta, tell me how long, how long
I'm gonna wait for you, baby, I've gotta see you since you been gone.

Roberta

Huddie Ledbetter

edited by John A. Lomax and Alan Lomax

Tempo: 100-120

Tuning: B, E, A, D, F#, B

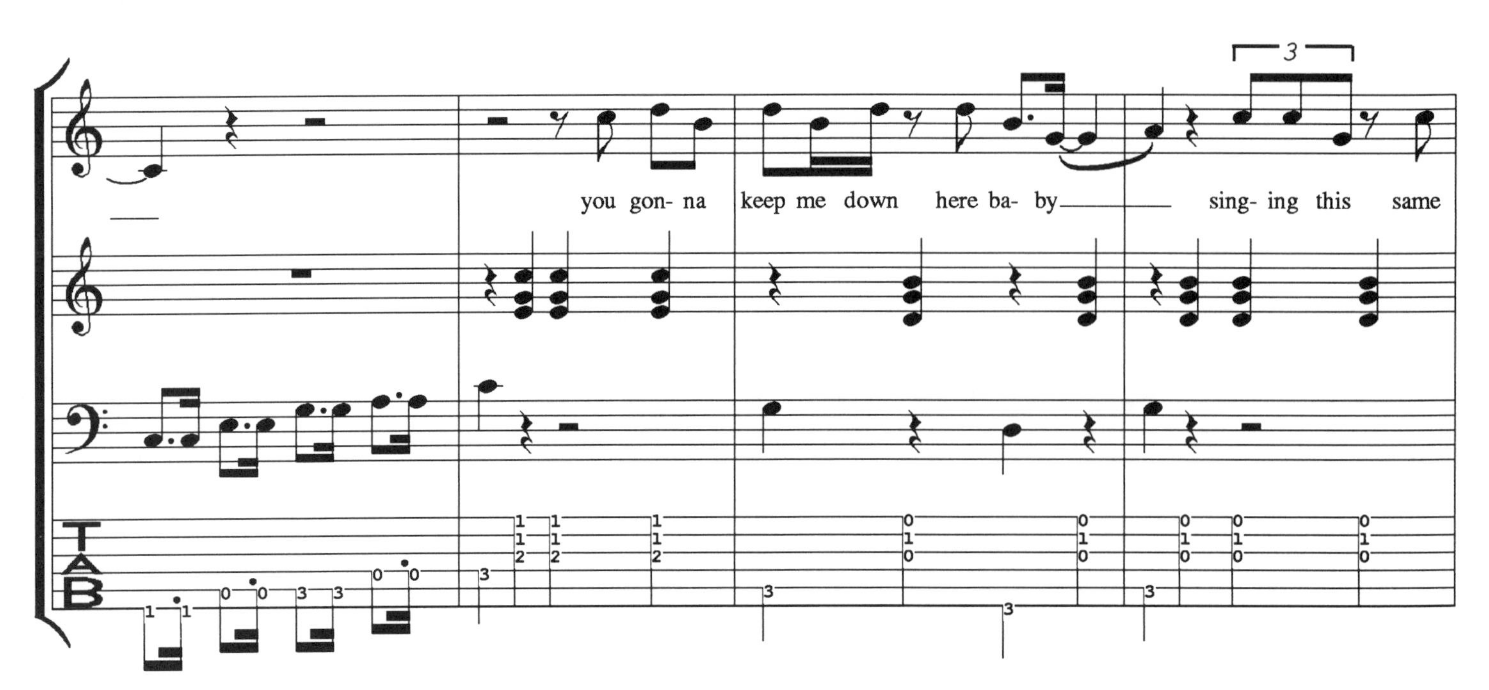
3
you gon- na
keep me down
here ba- by
sing- ing this
same

old
song
I'm

One of Lead Belly's trademarks was the insertion of a semi-shouted narration between sung choruses. This is uncommon among blues singers, although Blind Lemon sometimes used short spoken lead-ins to some of his recorded performances.

The following is from the spoken text of the Library of Congress recording:

"This man, he was likin' Roberta, an' Roberta was a li'l' brownskin woman with coal-black, wavy hair. This man was all the time hangin' 'roun' Roberta, wouldn' give her no peace an' no res'. She tried to get away from him. She got tired of seein' him, an' she went to runnin' on a steamboat down the Mississippi River. The man went off an' sat on the banks of the river where he know Roberta had to pass by. An' he look way up the river an' here what he said: 'I'm down on the river, settin' down on the groun'...'"

Good Mornin' Blues

Transcribed from 1940 RCA sessions available on *Leadbelly/Alabama Bound*, RCA CD 9600-2-R. Other Lead Belly CD recordings: *Lead Belly/Bourgeois Blues* (undated), Smithsonian Folkways 40045; *Lead Belly/Where Did You Sleep Last Night?* (1943 Asch sessions with Sonny Terry on harmonica), Smithsonian Folkways 40044; *Good Morning Blues* (1940 WNYC radio broadcast), Jazz Heritage Society 513464F; *Bunk & Leadbelly at New York Town Hall 1947* (with Bunk Johnson, New Orleans trumpet player), American Music AMCD-46.

(Spoken)
Now this is the blues.
Never was a white man had the blues
'Cause nothin' to worry about.
Now you lay down at night,
You roll from one side of the bed to the other all night long.
You can't sleep. What's the matter? The blues has got you.
You get up and sit on the side of the bed in the mornin'.
May have a sister and a brother, mother and father around,
But you don't want no talk out of 'em.
What's the matter? The blues got you.
Well, you go and put your feet under the table,
Look down in your plate, got everything you want to eat.
But you shake your head, you get up.
You say, "Lord, I can't eat and I can't sleep."
What's the matter? The blues got you.
They want to talk to you.
Here's what you got to tell 'em.

Chorus:
Good mornin' blues, blues how do you do? (2)
I'm doin' all right, good mornin', how are you?

I lay down last night, turnin' from side to side, oh
Turnin' from side to side.
I was not sick but I was just dissatisfied.

When I got up this mornin' with the blues walkin' 'round my bed,
Aaah with the blues walkin' 'round my bed,
I wouldn't eat my breakfast, blues was all in my bread. (Chorus)

Lord, a brown-skinned woman'll make a moon-eyed man go blind,
Aaah she would make a moon-eyed man go blind,
And a jet black woman'll make you take your time. (Chorus)

(additional verse from 1943 recording)
I sent for you yesterday.
Here you come a-walkin' today.
Got your mouth wide open,
You don't know what to say.

Good Mornin' Blues

Huddie Ledbetter

edited by Alan Lomax

Tempo: 110-120

Tuning: C#,F#,B,E,G#,C#

blues how do you— do—
I'm do-
T
A
B

— in' all right good morn-
in' how— are you—
T
A
B

Poor Howard

Transcribed from 1940 Library of Congress sessions now available on *Lead Belly/Gwine Dig A Hole To Put The Devil In*, Rounder CD 1045. Other Lead Belly recordings: *Lead Belly/In The Shadow Of The Gallows Pole*, Tradition CD 1018, *Leadbelly/Bourgeois Blues* and *Lead Belly Memorial Vols. 3 & 4*, Collectables CDs 5183 and 5604 (1939 Musicraft sessions). Additional Library of Congress recordings are included in two monologues on square dances or sooky jumps: *Lead Belly/Go Down Old Hannah*, Rounder CD 1099 and *Leadbelly/The Library of Congress Recordings*, Elektra boxed LP set EKL-301/2.

He was the first fiddler after Negroes got freed in slavery times. Po' Howard was a Negro, used to play for 'em at the sooky jumps and the number he played it was "Po' Howard, Po' Boy." ...Because they dance so fast, the music was so fast and the people had to jump, so they always called them sooky jumps... Sooky, well that's a cow – sometimes when you tell it "sooky, sooky, sooky", you know, sookin' the cow away.

Huddie Ledbetter, 1940

Old Howard's poor boy.
Old Howard's dead and gone.
Left me here to sing this song.

Left me here to sing this song. (3)
Who's been here since I've been gone? (2)

Pretty little girl with a red dress on. (2)
Pretty little girl with a red dress on, old Howard's poor boy.
Left me here to shout for joy
Old Howard's dead and gone.

Left me here to sing this song. (2)
Left me here to sing this song, old Howard's dead and gone.
Old Howard's poor boy, old Howard's poor boy.
Left me here to shout for joy, goodbye Howard, dead and gone.

(additional lyrics from Elektra Library of Congress recording)
Who's been here since I been gone
Big black man with a derby on,

The day I left my mother's home
The day I left my home
The day I left my father's door
The day I left my home
The day I left my friends (4)

Lead Belly Archives

Poor Howard

Huddie Ledbetter

edited by John A. Lomax and Alan Lomax

Tempo: 127-130

Tuning: B, E, A, D, F#, B

left me here to sing this song
left me here to sing this song

who's been here since I've been gone

who's been here since I've been gone

Green Corn

Transcribed from 1939 Musicraft sessions now available on *Lead Belly/In The Shadow Of The Gallows Pole*, Tradition CD 1018, *Leadbelly/Bourgeois Blues* and *Lead Belly Memorial Vols. 3 & 4*, Collectables CDs 5183 and 5604. Other CD recordings: *Lead Belly/Gwine Dig A Hole To Put The Devil In* (1940 Library of Congress sessions), Rounder 1045; *Lead Belly/Where Did You Sleep Last Night?* (Asch session possibly in June 1946), Smithsonian Folkways 40044. Another circa October 1946 Asch session with Woody Guthrie and Cisco Houston was released on *Take This Hammer/Leadbelly Legacy Number One*, Folkways 10" LP FA 2004.

Green corn is brand new moonshine whiskey and jimmy-john is a jug to hold it. This tune was most often played on the fiddle at square dances.

Lead Belly Archives

(Intro: Lead Belly tap dance)

(Chorus)
Green corn, green corn
Green corn, come along Cholly
Green corn, go and tell Polly
Green corn, green corn.

All I want in this creation
Little bit o' wife, big plantation
Two little boys to call me papa
One name Sop and one name Gravy.

(Chorus)
Green corn
Green corn, come along Cholly
Green corn, go and tell Polly
Green corn, come along Cholly
Green corn.

Two little boys call me papa
One name Sop and one name Gravy
One name Sop and one name Gravy
One gonna put up and the other gonna save it. *(Chorus)*

Stand around, stand around the jimmy-john. *(4) (Chorus)*

Wake snake, day's a breakin'
Peas in the pot and the hoecakes a-bakin'. *(Chorus)*

(alternate Chorus)
Stand around, stand around
Stand around the jimmy-john.

Green Corn

Huddie Ledbetter

edited by John A. Lomax and Alan Lomax

Tempo: 135-145

Tuning: B, E, A, D, F#, B

green corn
green corn
all I___ want this cre- a- tion___
3
lit- tle bit o' wife big plan- ta- tion
two lit- tle boys___ to call me pa- pa

one name Sop and one name Gra- vy___
green corn

green corn come a- long Chol- ly
green corn go and tell Pol- ly

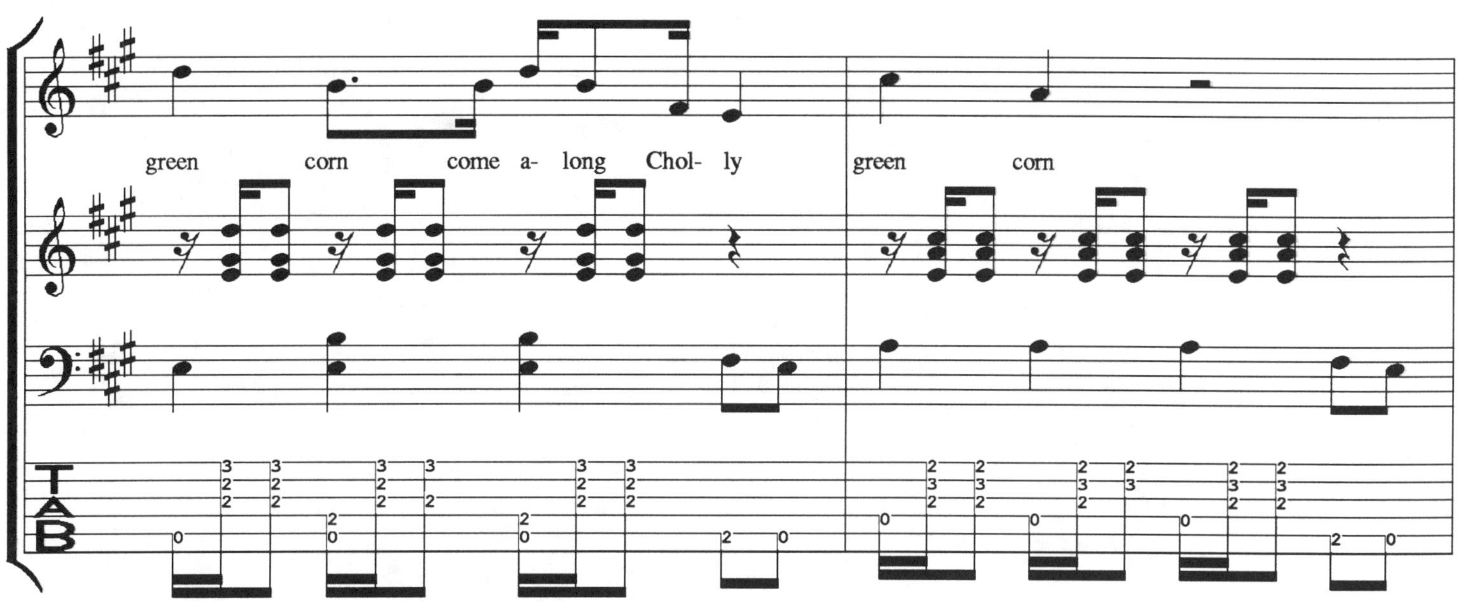
green corn come a- long Chol- ly
green corn

Lead Belly Archives

Lead Belly Archives

Little Children's Blues

(Children's Blues)

Transcribed from May 1944 Asch sessions now available on *Leadbelly Sings Folk Songs*, Smithsonian Folkways CD 40010. Another 1944 recording for Asch first released on the Stinson label is available on *Leadbelly/Party Songs & Sings and Plays*, Collectables CD 5609.

"These blues for little children - made about somebody that's goin' away and that's sad and that gives you the blues." Huddie Ledbetter

As I went down to the railroad track,
When that train comes a-rolling by,
I wave my hand at the girl that I love, my mama;
Hung down my head and I cry.

My mama she's gone, my mama she's gone,
And she left me to weep and moan.
She left me to weep and moan
Just to think about my poor mother is gone.

As I went down to the freight depot,
When that train comes a-rolling by,
I wave my hand at my mama that I love;
Hung down my head and I cry.

She's gone, she's gone, she's gone, she's gone,
And no crying won't bring her back.
Anymore that I boo-hoo,
She's going further down the track.

(additional verses from another recording)
She's gone, she's gone, she's gone, she's gone,
And no crying won't bring her back.
She's the onliest mother that I ever did love
Going down that railroad track.

As I went down to the freight depot
And I looked upon this sign,
Thinking about the onliest mother I have in this world,
And I couldn't help from hanging my head and crying.

It was fare you well, it was fare you well,
And she's gone, she's gone, she's gone.
She's gone down that lonesome railroad track,
And she's left me here to sing this song.

Little Children's Blues

(Children's Blues)

Huddie Ledbetter

Tempo: 85-95
Tuning: X, X, G, D, G, D
Do not play fifth and sixth course

train comes a- roll- ing by I wave my
hand at the girl that I love (my ma- ma) Hung
down my head and I cry My

Lead Belly Archives

Lead Belly and dancing children, New York City, mid-1940s Lead Belly Archives

Ha, Ha, Thisaway

Transcribed from 1942 Asch recording available on *Lead Belly/Where Did You Sleep Last Night?*, Smithsonian Folkways CD 40044. Other Lead Belly recordings: *Lead Belly/Nobody Knows The Trouble I've Seen* (1935 Library of Congress sessions), Rounder CD 1098; *Lead Belly/Party Songs & Sings and Plays* (1944 Asch sessions formerly released on Stinson LPs), Collectables CD 5609.

This is little children play song. They make the ring and they sing, they put one inside of the ring and as they go round and sing, hold to each other's hands, they sing "Ha, ha, thisaway" and "ha, ha, thataway" and the one in the ring, he gonna jump thataway, and when he jump thataway, the others gonna jump on 'round the ring, and he gonna jump to the one and he gonna catch one by the hand and put him in the ring and he gonna get out in the ring with the other children and go around and here's what they sing. Huddie Ledbetter

Chorus:
Ha, ha, thisaway, ha, ha, thataway,
Ha, ha, thisaway, then oh then.

When I was a little boy, little boy, little boy,
When I was a little boy, twelve years old,
Papa went and left me, left me, left me,
Papa went and left me, so I was told. (Chorus)

Mama come and got me, she got me, got me,
Mama come and got me to save my soul.
Mama never whup me, whup me, whup me,
Mama never whup me so I was told. (Chorus)

I went to school, went to school, went to school, boys,
I went to school when I was twelve years old.
Obeyed the rules, the rules, the rules, boys,
Obeyed the rules as I was told. (Chorus)

I went to a teacher, teacher, teacher,
I went to a teacher to save my soul.
Teacher was a preacher, preacher, preacher,
Teacher was a preacher so I was told. (Chorus)

I learned my lesson, lesson, lesson,
I learned my lesson to save my soul.
Wasn't that a blessin', blessin', blessin',
Wasn't that a blessin' so I was told? (Chorus)

(verses from Library of Congress recording)
I went a-walkin'...when I was eleven years old.
I was a-talkin'...so I was told.

I went a-ridin'...when I was eleven years old.
I was a-drivin'...when I was twelve years old.

I was writing...to save my soul.
I was typing...so I was told.

(Alternate chorus)
Ho, ho, thisaway, ha, ha, thataway,
Ho, ho, thisaway, then oh then.

Ha, Ha, Thisaway

Huddie Ledbetter

edited by John A. Lomax and Alan Lomax

Tempo: 90-115

Tuning: C, F, A#, D#, G, C

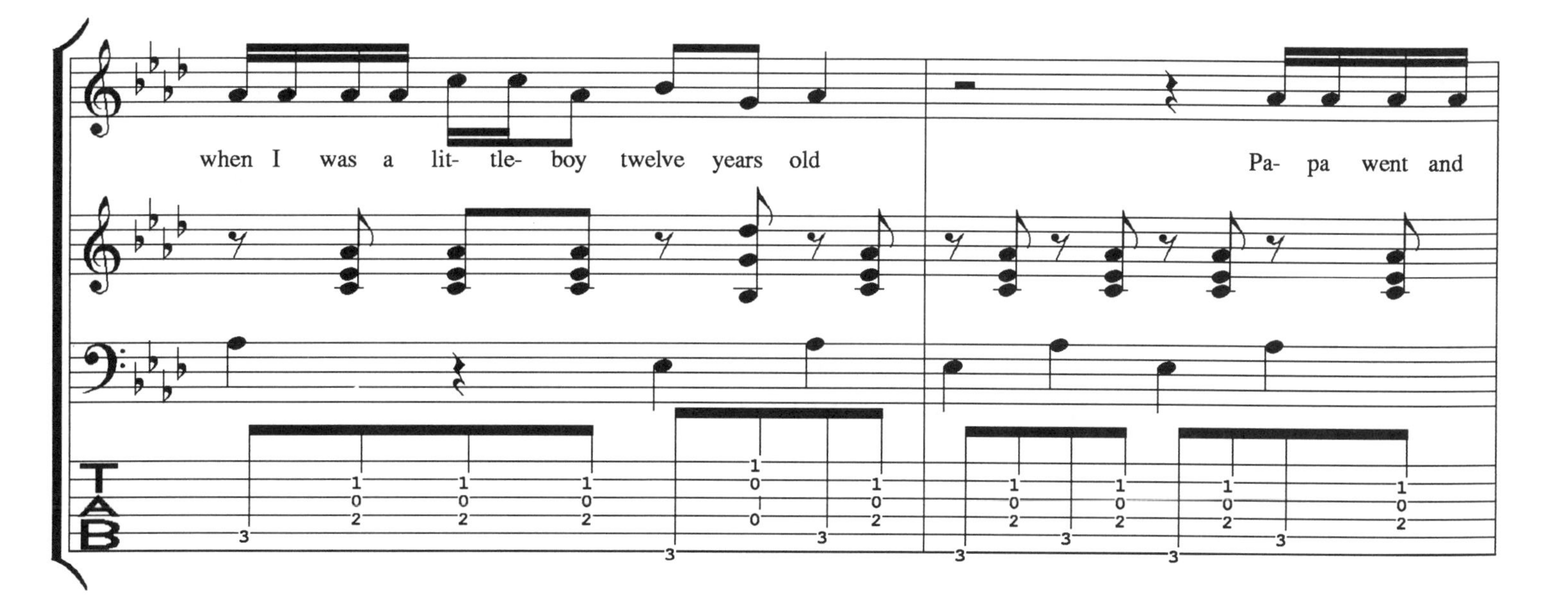
when I was a lit- tle- boy twelve years old
Pa- pa went and

left me left me left me Pa- pa went and
left me so I was told Ha ha

this- a- way ha ha that- a way ha ha
this- a way then oh then

Red River

Transcribed from unissued 1935 American Record Company sessions released on *Leadbelly*, Columbia CD SK 30035. Other CD recordings: *Lead Belly/Midnight Special* (1935 Library of Congress sessions), Rounder 1044; *Lead Belly Memorial Vols. 3 & 4* (1944 recording originally released on Stinson LP), Collectables 5604.

The Red River runs through Shreveport, Louisiana.

Tell me which-a way do the Red River run? (2)
Ah, some folks say it runs, runs from sun to sun.

Some folks say it runs from sun to sun
Way down in Louisiana where the work was done.

Tell me, pretty mama, which-a way you goin'?
If you can't tell me, that's gonna be your run.

I got up this mornin', hung all around my brown
'Cause she told me which-a way the Red River was a-runnin' down.

Would you take a poor old, old slave like me?
I left my baby, you gonna let me be.

(additional verses from Library of Congress recording)
I'm gonna tell you somethin', baby, and that ain't no joke,
That the woman I'm lovin' every morning so,
Last woman I'm lovin' every street she cross.

Some folks tell me, Lord, it was not so
But that Red River's runnin' every way I go.

(extra verses from 1944 recording)
Red River it's so deep and wide,
Well, I can't get a letter from the other side.

The old folks always tell me it runs from east to west,
And I always didn't believe them, they didn't know the best.

Red River

Huddie Ledbetter

Tempo: 105-130

Tuning: B, E, A, D, F#, B

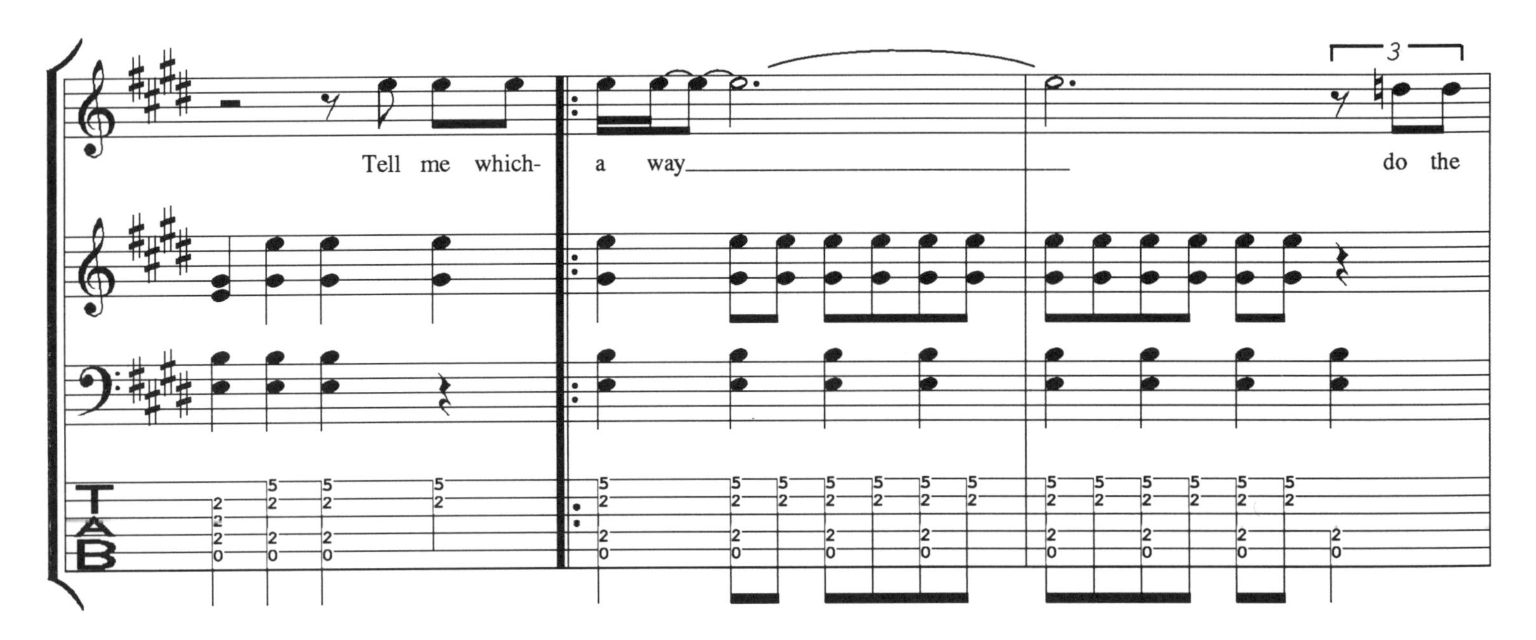
Tell me which- a way do the

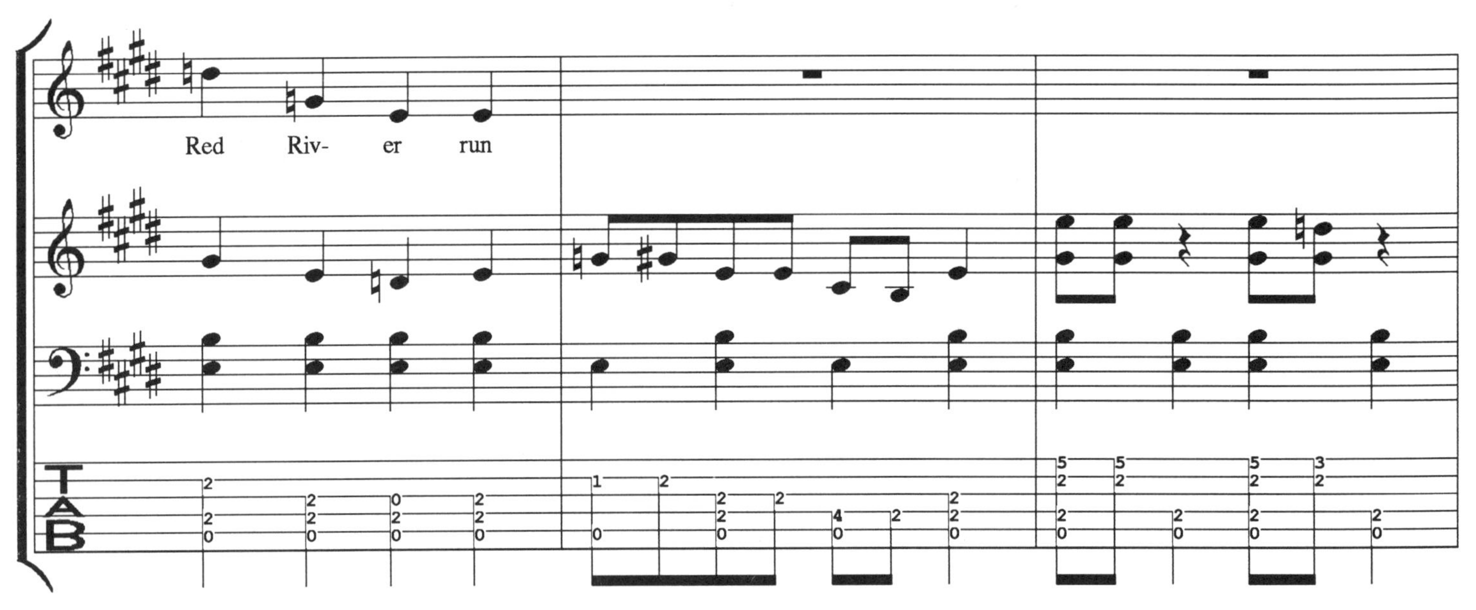
Red Riv- er run

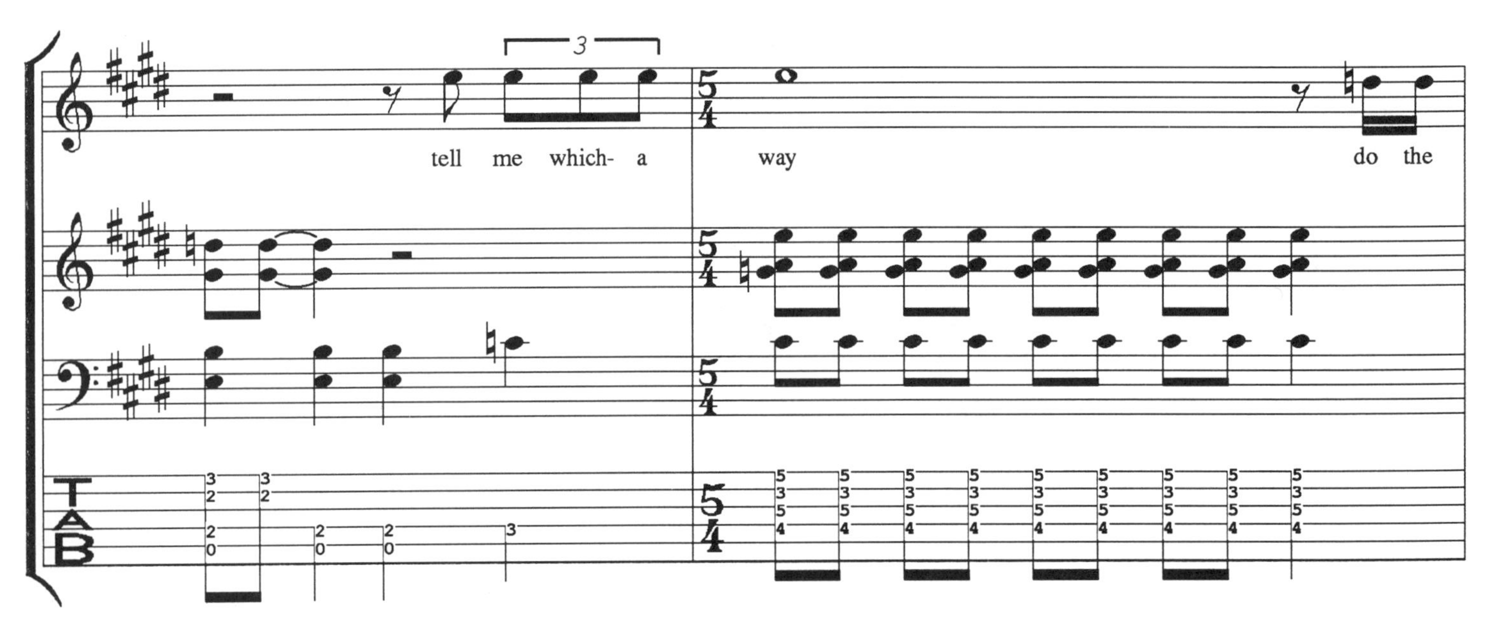
tell me which- a way do the

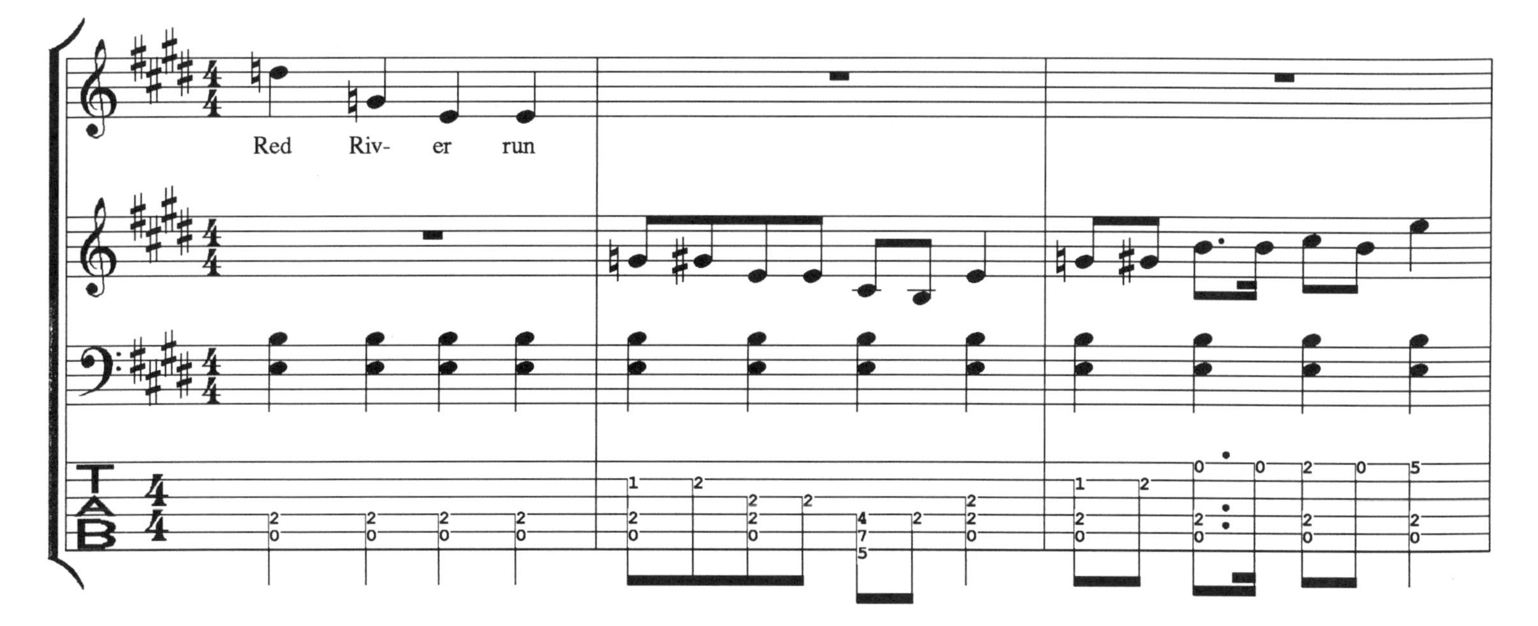
Red Riv- er run

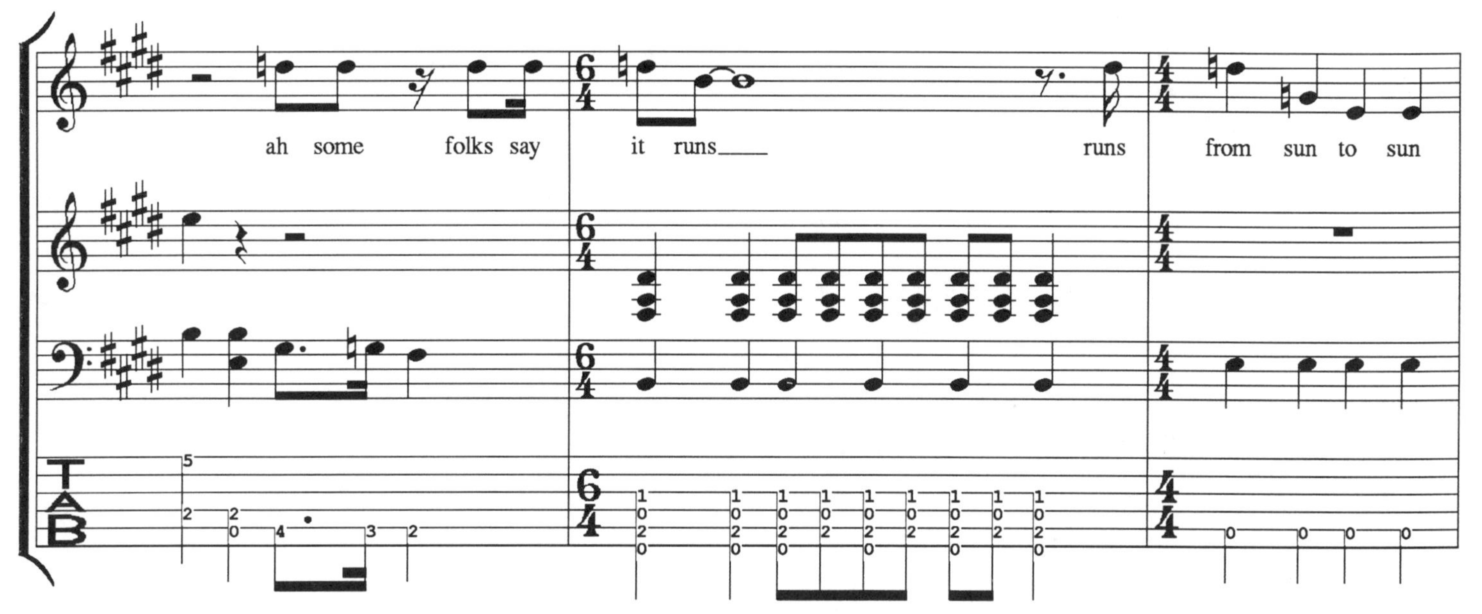
ah some folks say
it runs___ runs
from sun to sun

Some folks say

Shorty George

Transcribed from 1935 American Record Company sessions released on *Leadbelly/King of the 12-String Guitar*, Columbia CD CK46776. Other Lead Belly recordings: *Leadbelly–Blind Willie McTell/Masters of the Country Blues* (alternate take from the same ARC sessions with additional verses), Biograph CD 144; *Lead Belly/Nobody Knows The Trouble I've Seen* (1935 Library of Congress sessions), Rounder CD 1098; *Lead Belly/Where Did You Sleep Last Night?* (1941 WNYC radio broadcast), Smithsonian Folkways CD 40044; *Lead Belly's Last Sessions* (1948), Smithsonian Folkways CD boxed set 40068/71.

Shorty George was a short train that brought families to visit Sugarland Prison and unfortunately took them away to the prisoners' regret.

Well, Shorty George ain't no friend of mine; (2)
He keeps a-taking all the women, leaving the men behind.

I went to the depot, looked up on the sign;
Oh, the train she ride took my girl 'fore time.

I'm gonna ask the captain, "Captain, if you don't care,
I'm gonna take my baby and bring her right back here."

Shorty George traveling through the land,
Don't take all the women, take some woman's man.

Some got six months, some got two and three years,
But there's so many good men got lifetime here.

Shorty George done been here and gone,
Left so many good men a long way from home.

(additional verses on Biograph CD)
I want to tell you, captain, it's a dirty shame,
Shorty George got my woman, have me all in vain.

Well, I can't do nothing, hon', but wave my hand,
Got my lifetime sentence down in Sugarland.

I got something to tell you, don't let it make you mad,
I ain't got long down here, honey, you heard I had.

(additional verses from Library of Congress sessions)
It was nineteen hundred and thirty-four,
My baby she left me standing in the door.

Lord, I went to the depot, turning round and round
Looking for my baby, she was Alabama bound.

Shorty George done been here and gone,
Lord, he's taken my woman to a world unknown.

Lay down at night, Lord, dreaming in my sleep
That I saw my baby making a before-day creep.

Got up this morning, Lord, I fold my arms,
Lord, too late to holler when the train was gone.

Taken so many women, Lord, from the men
And there's so many good men, lifetime in the pen.

Shorty George

Huddie Ledbetter

edited by John A. Lomax and Alan Lomax

Tempo: 125-145

Tuning: C, F, A#, D#, G, C

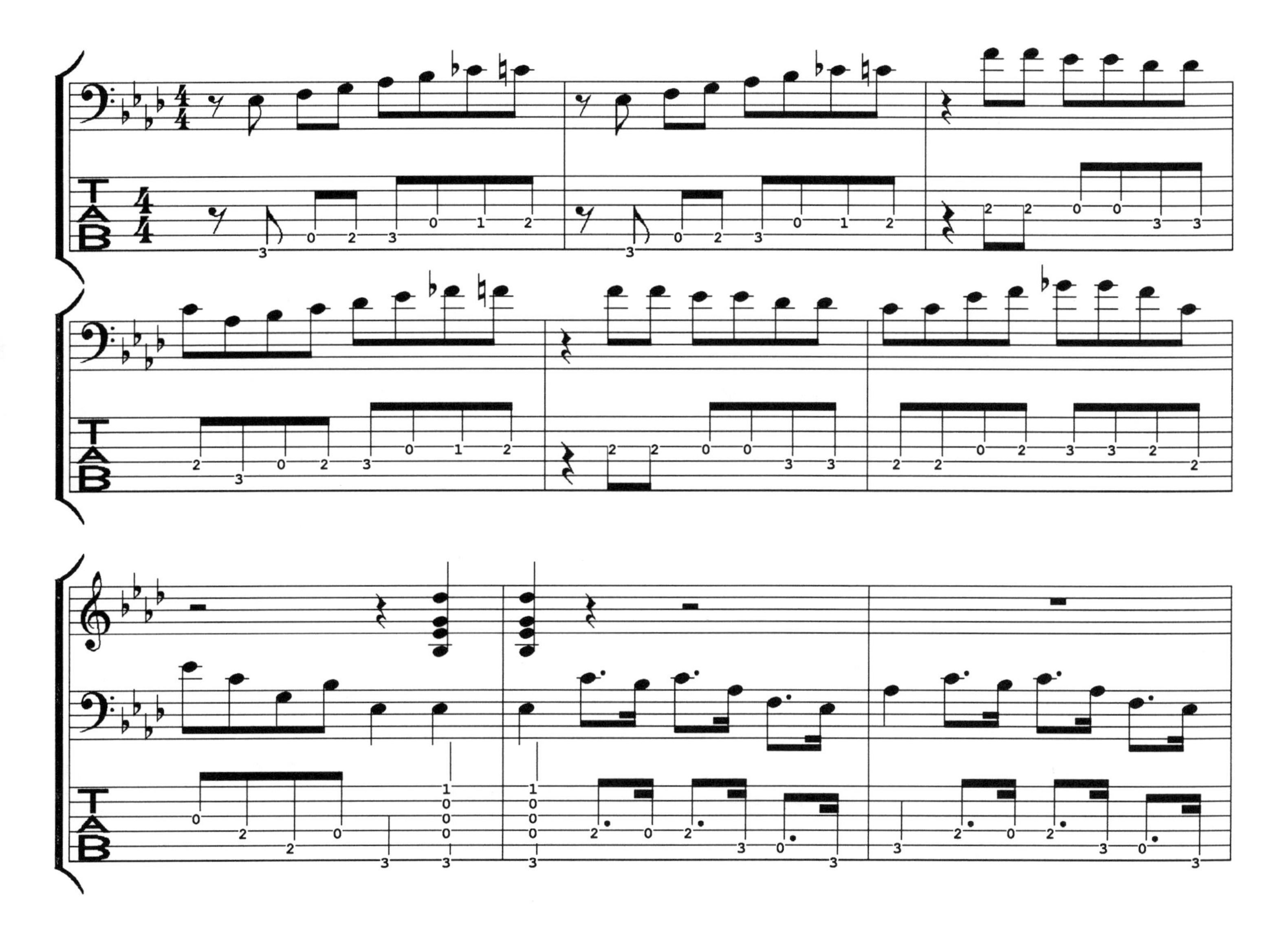

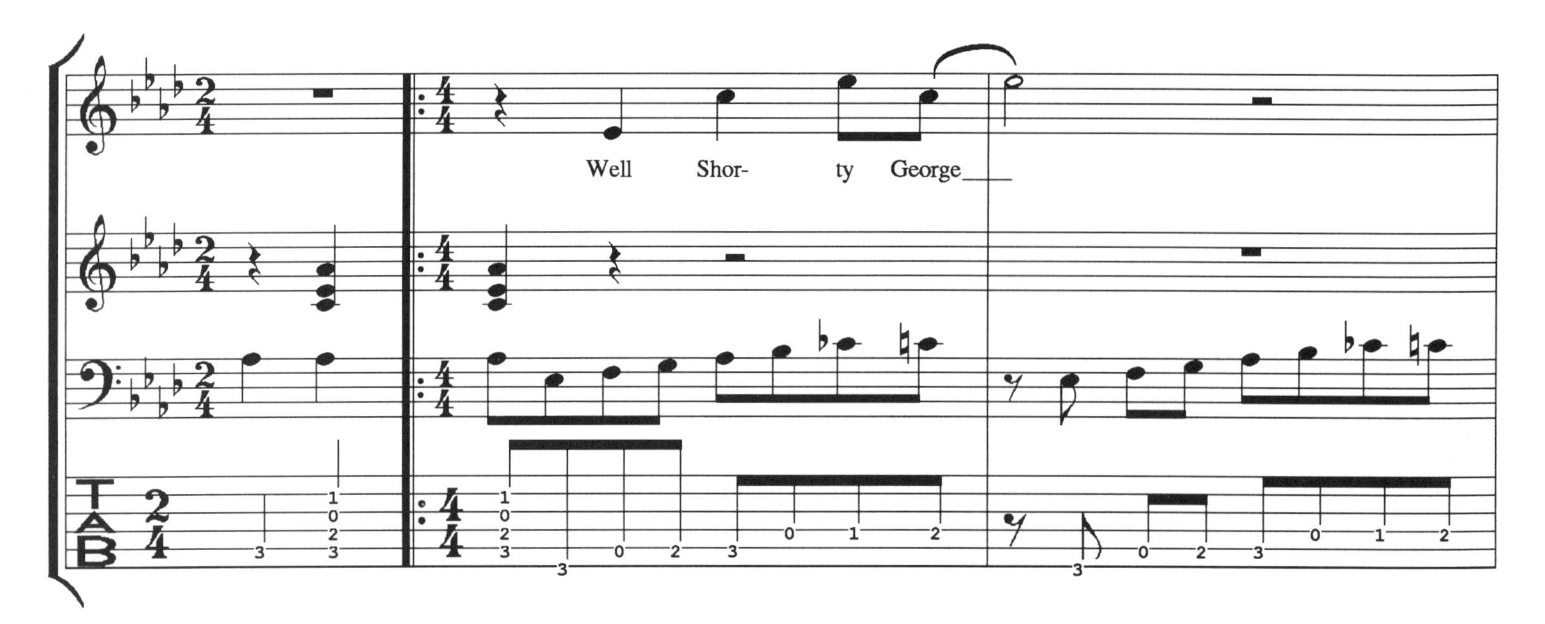
Well Shor- ty George

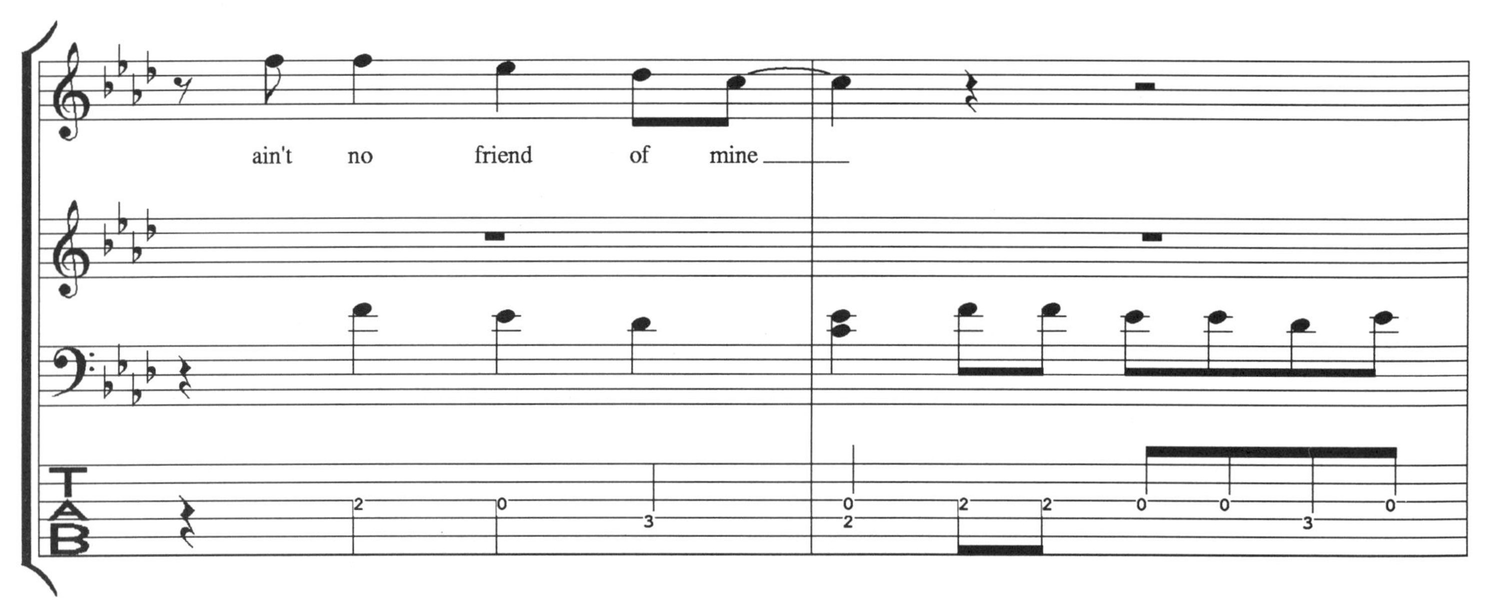
ain't no friend of mine

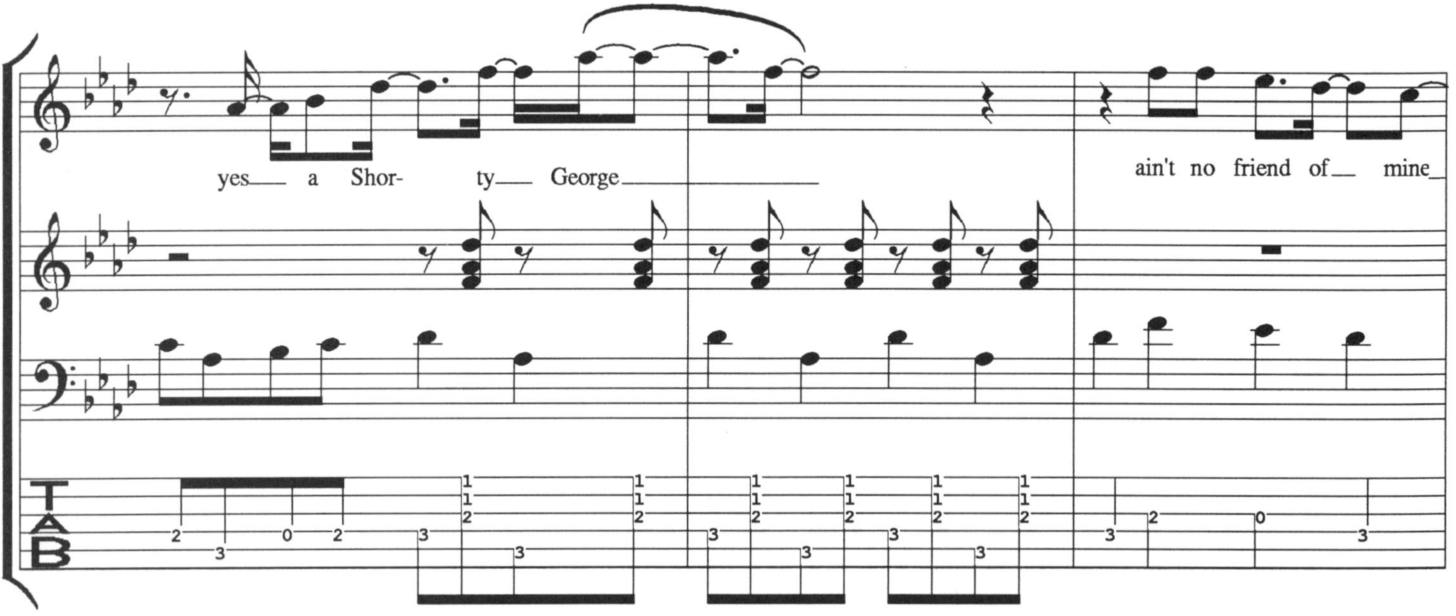
yes a Shor- ty George
ain't no friend of mine

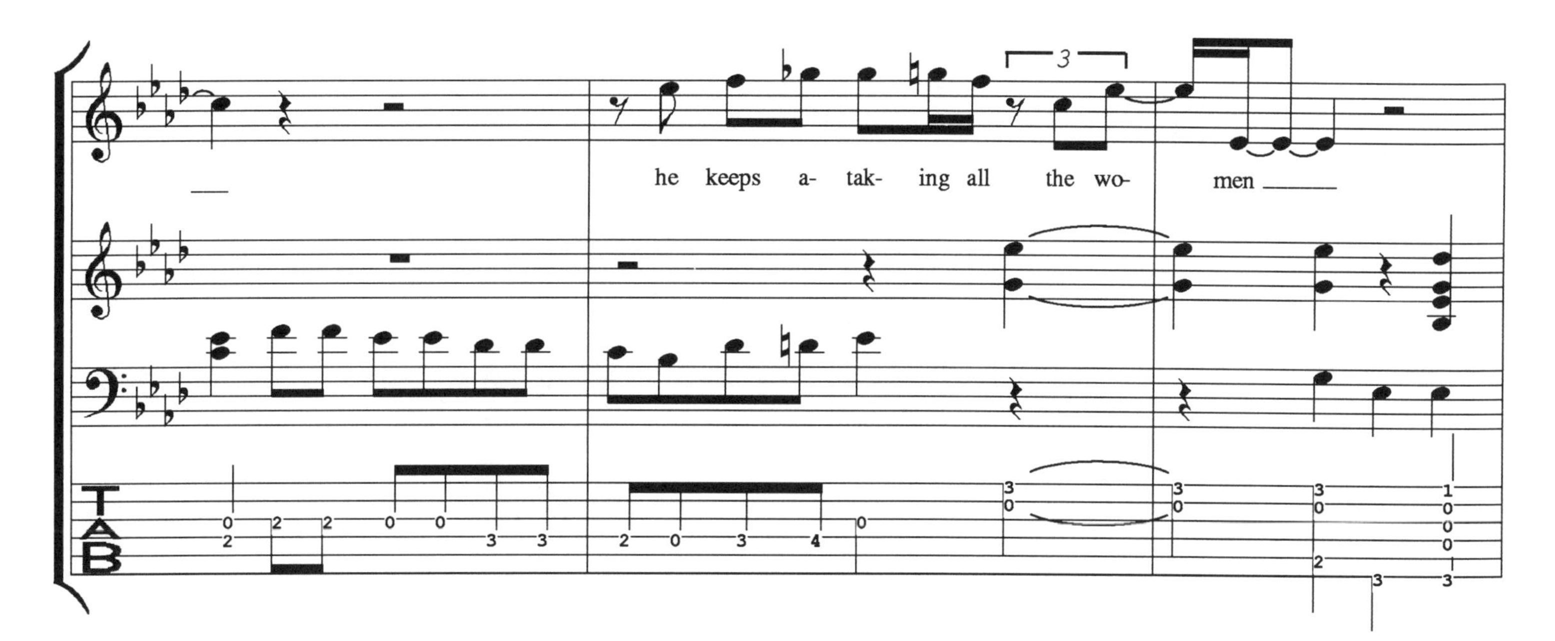
he keeps a- tak- ing all the wo- men
3

leav- ing the men be- hind.

Goodnight, Irene

Transcribed from 1943 Asch sessions now available on *Lead Belly/Where Did You Sleep Last Night?*, Smithsonian Folkways CD 40044. Other Lead Belly CD recordings: *Lead Belly/Midnight Special* (1935 Library of Congress sessions), Rounder 1044; *Lead Belly/Goodnight Irene* (1939 Musicraft sessions), Tradition 1006; *Lead Belly's Last Sessions* (1948), Smithsonian Folkways boxed set 40068/71.

Lead Belly's most famous song was a 1950 #1 hit by the Weavers and also had top ten recordings by such artists as Frank Sinatra, Jo Stafford, Red Foley and Ernest Tubb.

Irene, goodnight, Irene, goodnight.
Goodnight, Irene, goodnight, Irene.
*I kiss you in my dreams.**

Photograph: Carlo Pappolla Collection Lead Belly Archives

Sometimes I live in the country,
Sometimes I live in town.
Sometimes I have a great notion
Jumping into the river and drown.

Stop rambling and stop gambling,
Quit staying out late at night.
Go home to your wife and your family,
Sit down by the fireside bright.

(*verses from other recordings*)
I asked your mother for you;
She told me that you was too young.
I wish to the Lord that I never seen your face,
I'm sorry you ever was born.

I love Irene, God knows I do,
Love her till the sea runs dry.
If Irene turns her back on me,
I'm gonna take morphine and die.

You caused me to weep and you caused me to moan,
You caused me to leave my home.
Last word I heared her say,
"I want you to sing me a song."

Last Saturday night I got married,
Me and my wife settled down.
Now me and my wife have parted,
Gonna take me a stroll uptown.

*Popular song version: I'll see you in my dreams.

Goodnight, Irene

Huddie Ledbetter

John A. Lomax

Tempo: 115-120

Tuning: C, F, A#, D#, G, C

night I- rene good night I- rene I

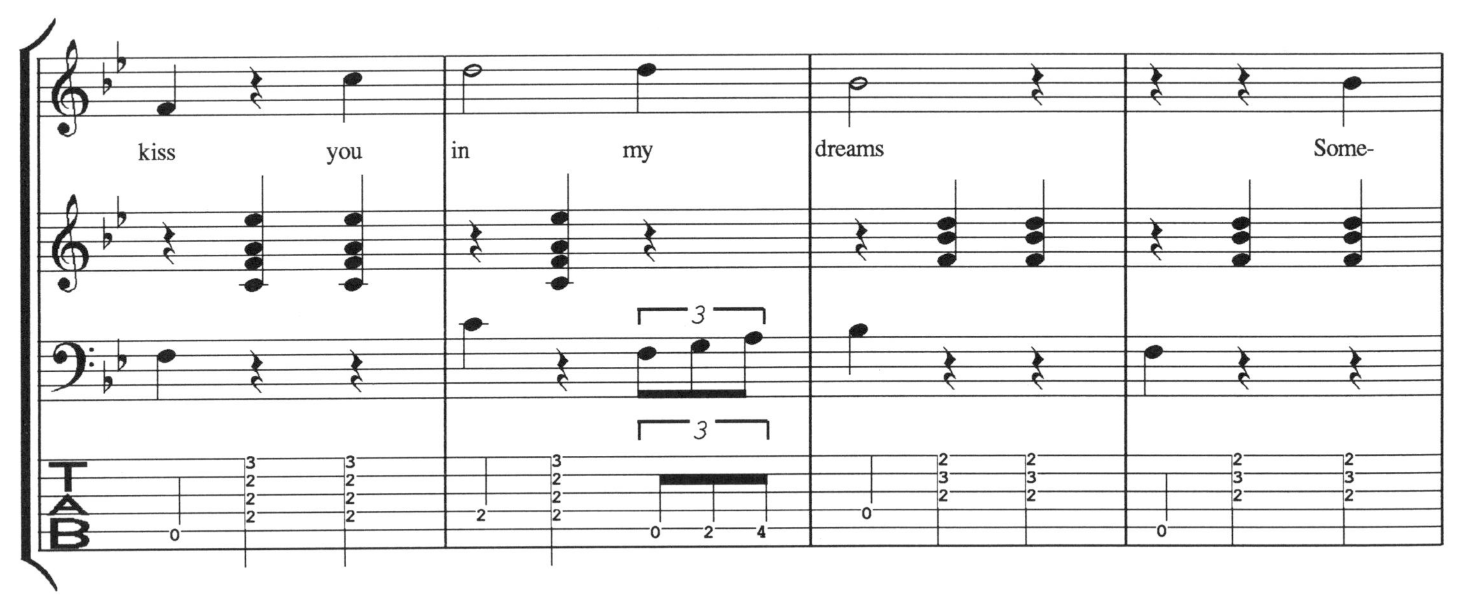
kiss you in my dreams Some-

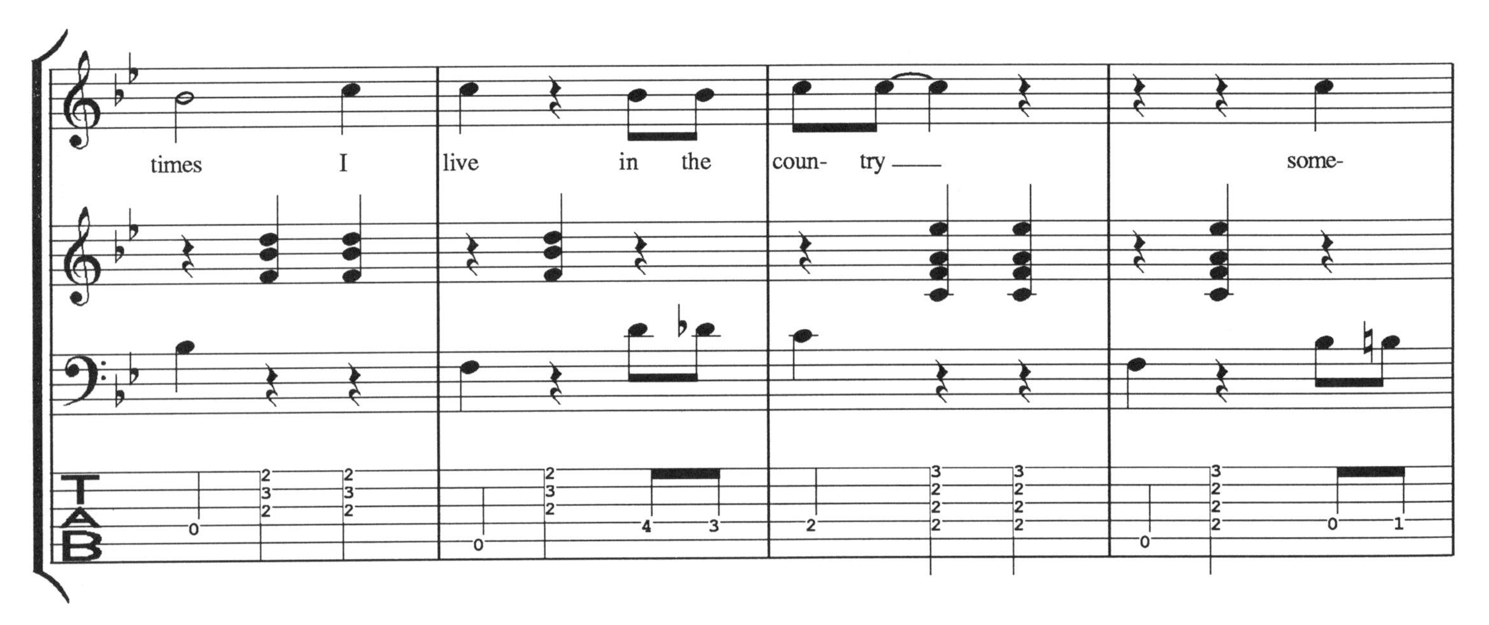
times I live in the coun- try some-

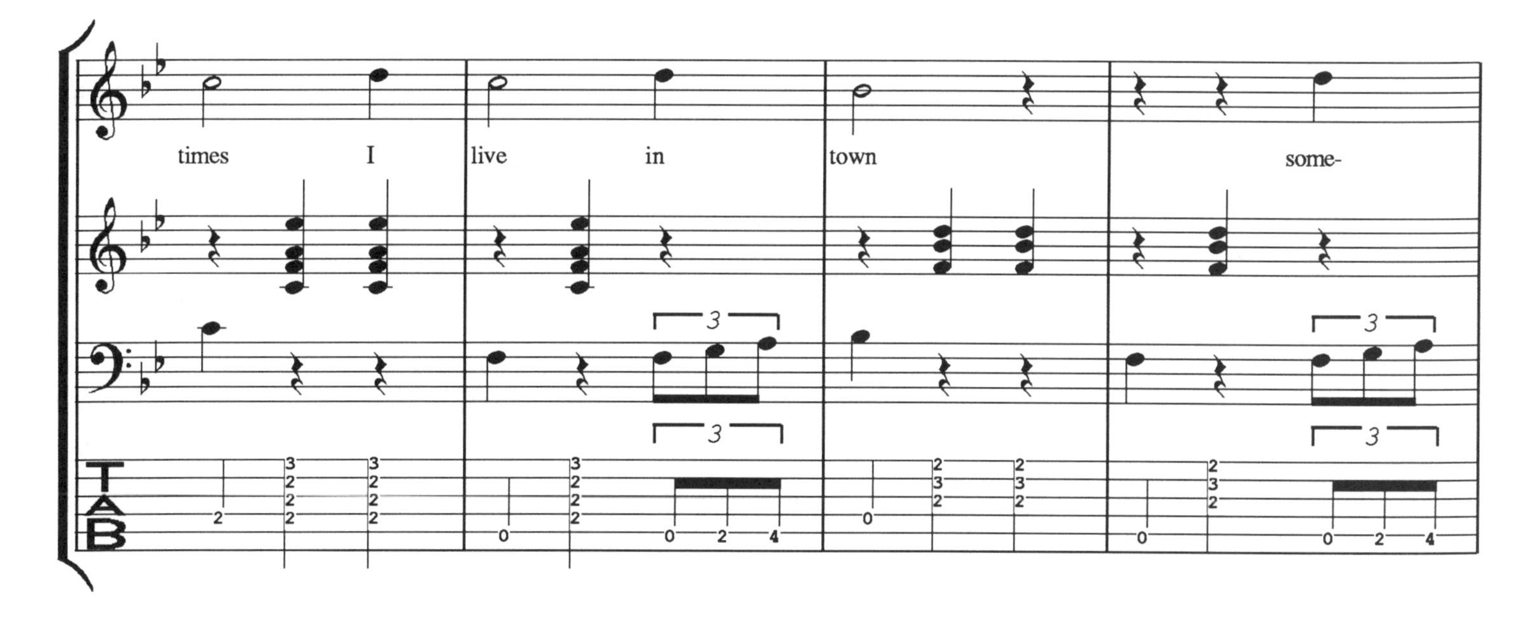
times I live in town some-
3
3

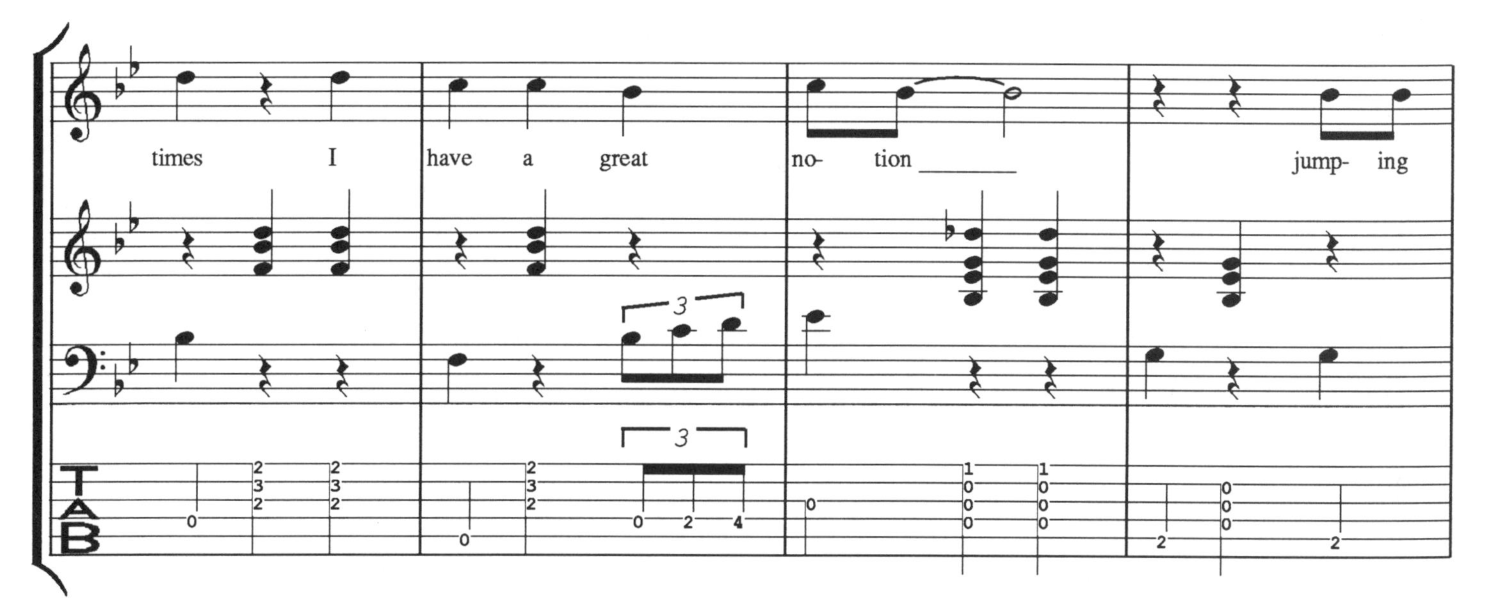
times I have a great no- tion jump- ing
3
3

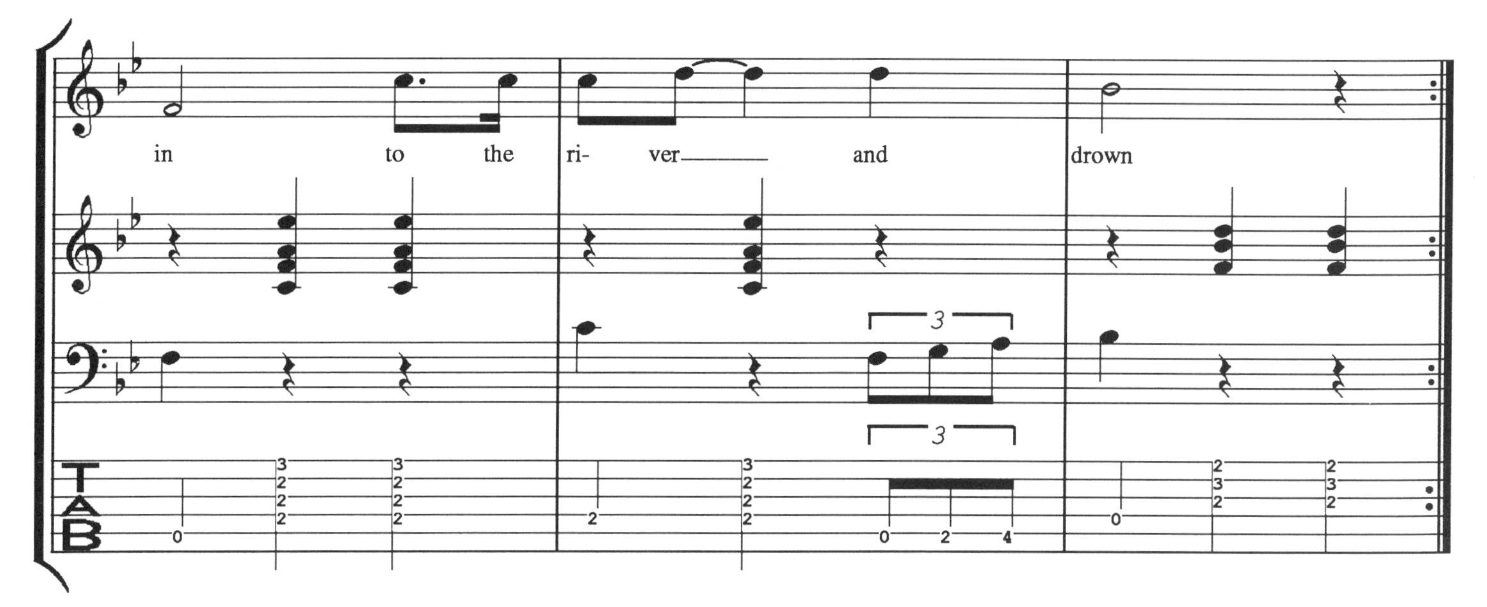
in to the ri- ver and drown
3
3

Leavin' Blues

Transcribed from October 1944 Capitol Records sessions *Leadbelly*, Capitol LP T1821 (under the title "Grasshoppers In My Pillow"). Lead Belly CD recordings: *Lead Belly/Let It Shine On Me* (1940 Library of Congress sessions), Rounder 1046; *Lead Belly/Where Did You Sleep Last Night?* (1941 WNYC radio program), Smithsonian Folkways 40044; *Lead Belly/Bourgeois Blues* (1947 a cappella recording), Smithsonian Folkways 40045. 1947 unreleased Musicraft sessions with verses unrecorded elsewhere were available on a bonus CD from Omega Records for a short time in 1994, and we have included them here. *Lead Belly's Last Sessions* includes a song titled "Leavin' Blues" which is actually "My Baby Left Me."

Lead Belly had this to say about "Leavin' Blues": *"Now this is the leavin' blues. What I mean it was leavin' time. This man had lived with a woman twenty years and he was working for the T.P.S. shop. And when he come home that evenin'...his time to come home was five o'clock...she got behind the door and just as he walked to the yard gate to come in, she jumped out from behind the door and throwed up both hands. She say, "You can't come in here no more." He say, "What's the matter?" She say, "I don't want you." He say, "Can I get my clothes?" She says, "Naw, you can't come." He turned around and that gave him the blues."*

Yes, I'm leaving in the morning, mama, but I don't know whoro to go (2)
'Cause the woman I've been living with for twenty years, mama,
says she don't want me no more.

Rather see my coffin comin', mama, Lordy, Lordy, in my back door
Than to have that good lookin' woman tell me to my face, mama,
that she couldn't use me no more.

I got grasshoppers in my pillow, baby, I got crickets all in my meal,
I got tacks in my shoes, mama, and they are stickin' in my heel.

(additional verses from 1940 recording)
I feel like walkin', mama, and I feel like lyin' down,
I would get drunk right now, baby, but there ain't no wine around.

I got holes in my pockets, baby, I got patches on my pants,
I'm behind in my house rent, mama; landlord, he want it all in advance.

Papa may be crazy this time, Papa ain't nobody's fool,
Before I stand the doggone way you're carrying on, baby,
go to buckin' like a Georgia mule.

(additional verses from Musicraft recording)
I'm leavin', leavin' on that mornin' train
Catch the mornin' train if you want to hear me sing.

Did you ever wake up in a big bed by yourself
Can't get the one you been lovin', you don't want nobody else.

I woke up this mornin', I found my baby gone
I was so mistreated, but I couldn't let on.

Oh Miss Alice, oh Miss Alice, oh Miss Alice, oh,
I got up this mornin' and I could not lay back down,
I was lookin' right at her, Lord she was standin' in her wedding gown.

I was late last night when I made my ride
I woke up this morning, my baby right by my side.

Leavin' Blues

Huddie Ledbetter

edited by Alan Lomax

Tempo: 110-120

Tuning: B, E, A, D, F#, B

Yes I'm
leav- in' in the morn- ing ma- ma

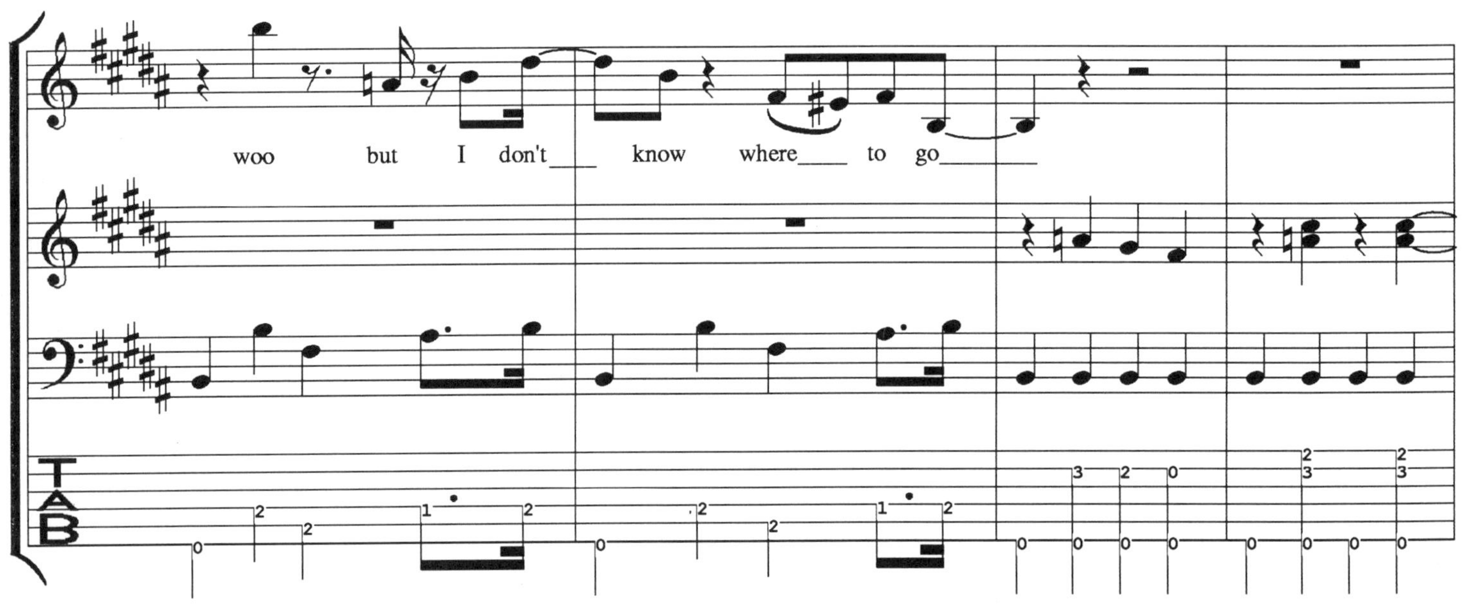
woo but I don't know where to go

I'm leav- ing in the
morn- ing ma- ma
but I don't know

where to go
'cause the wo- man I've
3

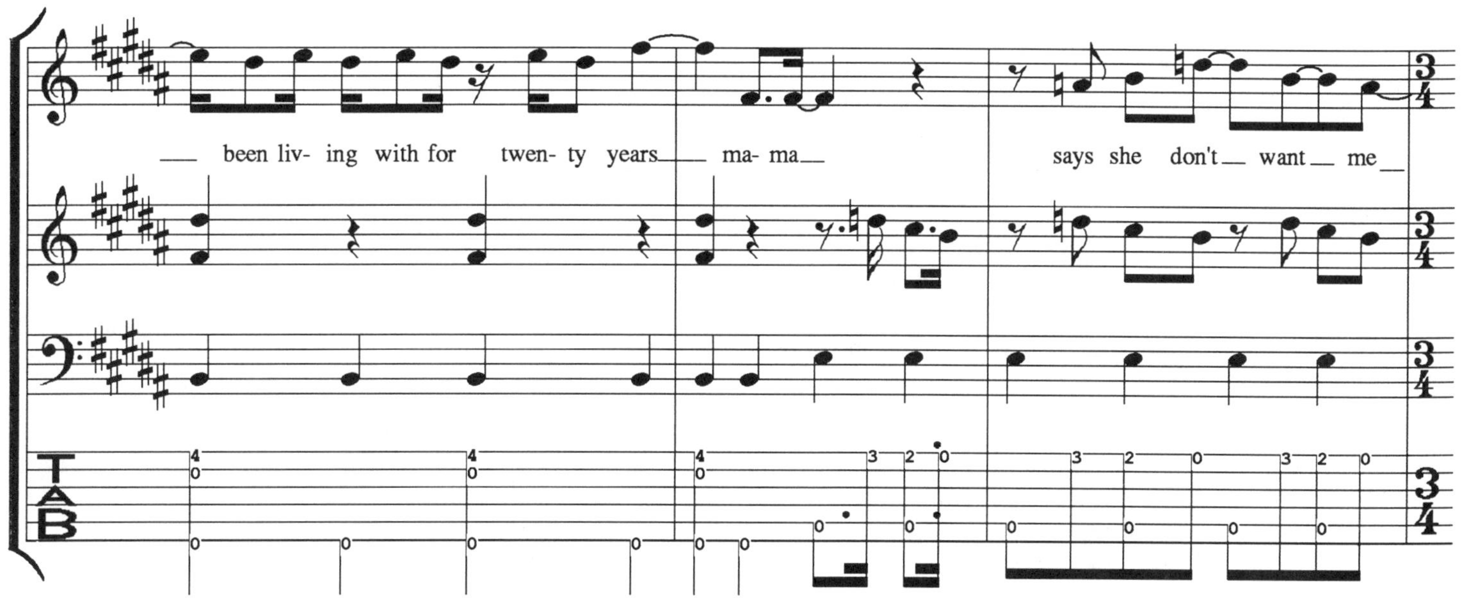
been liv- ing with for twen- ty years mama- ma
says she don't want me

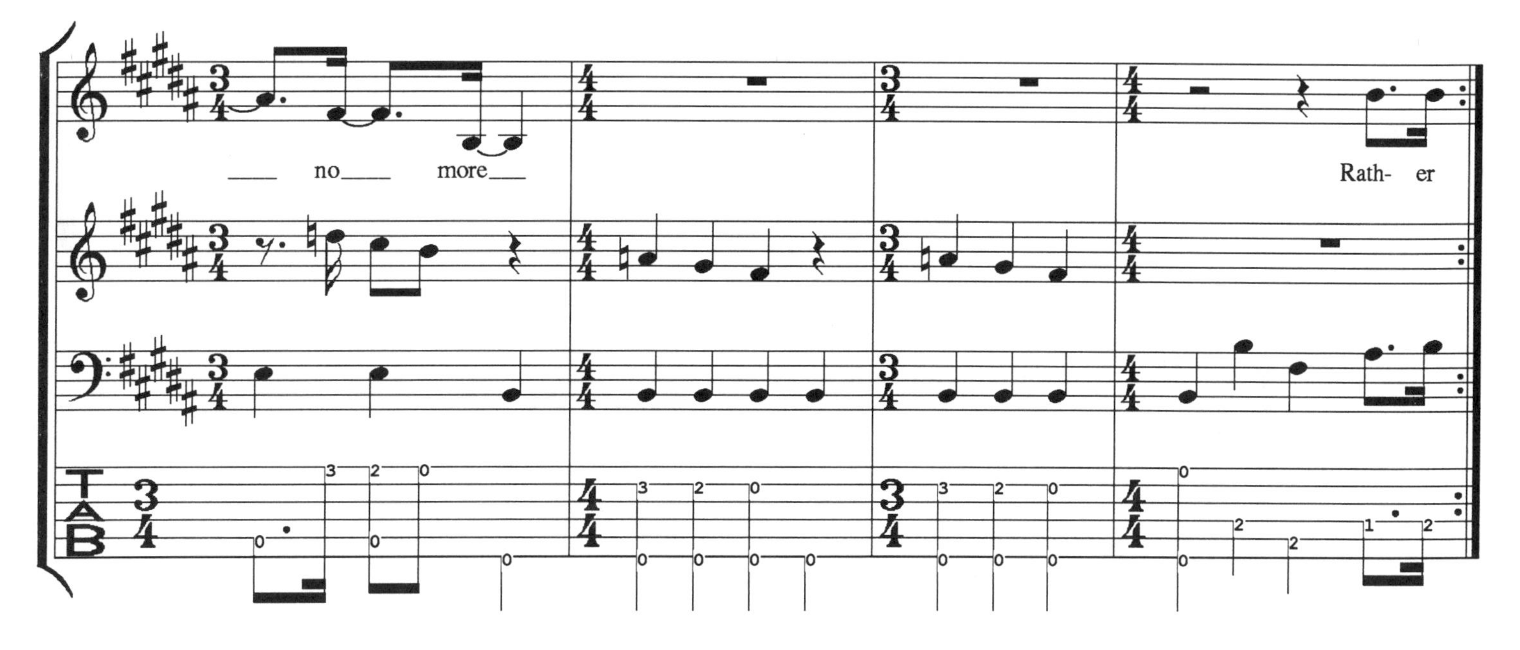
no more
Rath- er

The Gallis Pole

Transcribed from 1939 Musicraft sessions available on *Leadbelly/Bourgeois Blues*, Collectables CD 5183 and *Lead Belly/In the Shadow of the Gallows Pole*, Tradition CD 1018. Other CD recordings: *Lead Belly/ Gwine Dig a Hole to Put the Devil In* (1938 Library of Congress sessions), Rounder 1045; *Lead Belly/ Bourgeois Blues* (1948 radio broadcast recorded by Frederic Ramsey, Jr.), Smithsonian Folkways 40045.

Recent recordings: Alvin Youngblood Hart; Ben Andrews and the Blue Rider Trio.

Lead Belly's song was inspired by the Child ballad "The Maid Freed from the Gallows" about the ancient practice of prisoners buying their way free from hanging.

Father, did you bring me any silver?*
Father, did you bring me any gold?
What did you bring me, dear father,
To keep me from the gallis pole?
Yeah, what did you,
Yeah, what did you,
What did you bring me, keep me from gallis pole?

Son, I brought you some silver,
Son, I brought you some gold,
Son, I brought you everything
Keep you from the gallis pole.
Yes, I brought it,
Yes, I brought it,
I brought you to keep you from the gallis pole.

**In succeeding verses substitute mother, wife, friend.*

(alternate verse from 1948 radio broadcast and Library of Congress recording)
I never brought you no silver,
I never brought you no gold,
Just come by to see you
Hung up from the gallis pole.
"Lord, I thought it,
Yes, I thought it,
You would come see me hangin' from the gallis pole."

Gallis Pole

Huddie Ledbetter

edited by Alan Lomax

Tempo: 115-125

Tuning: C, F, A#, D#, G, C

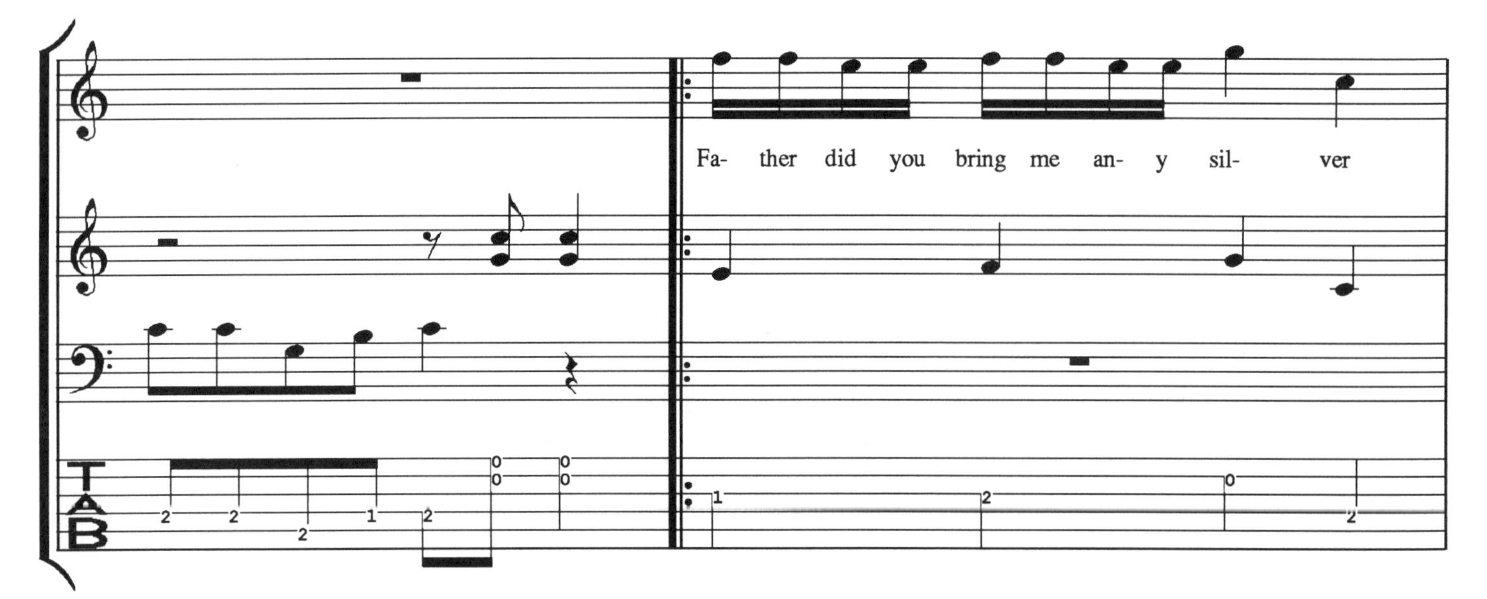
Fa- ther did you bring me an- y sil- ver

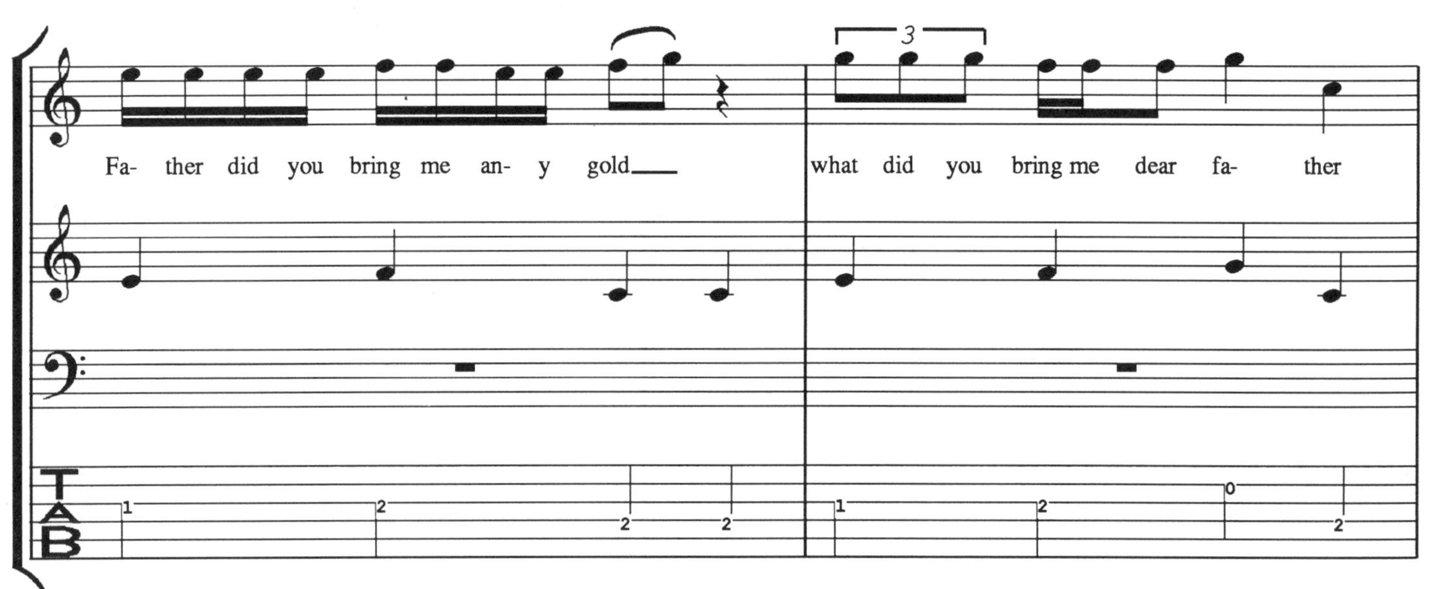
Fa- ther did you bring me an- y gold
what did you bring me dear fa- ther

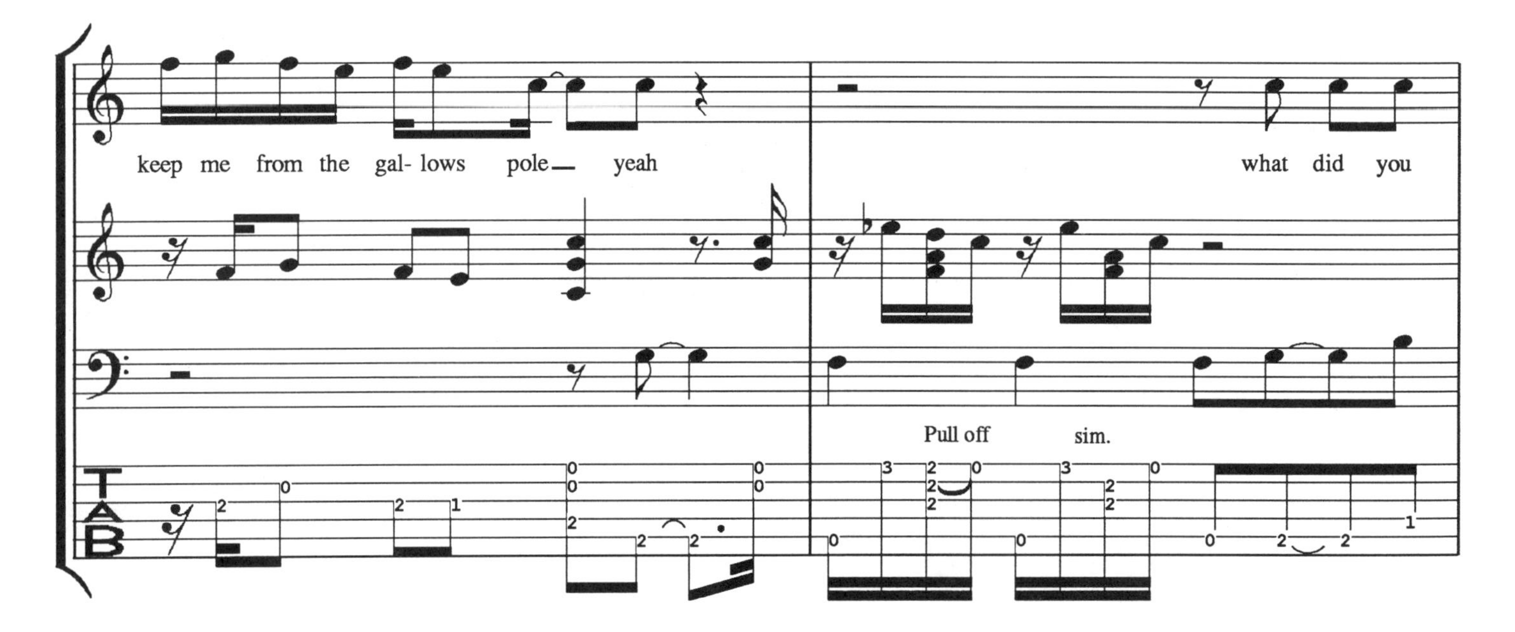
keep me from the gal- lows pole yeah
what did you
Pull off
sim.

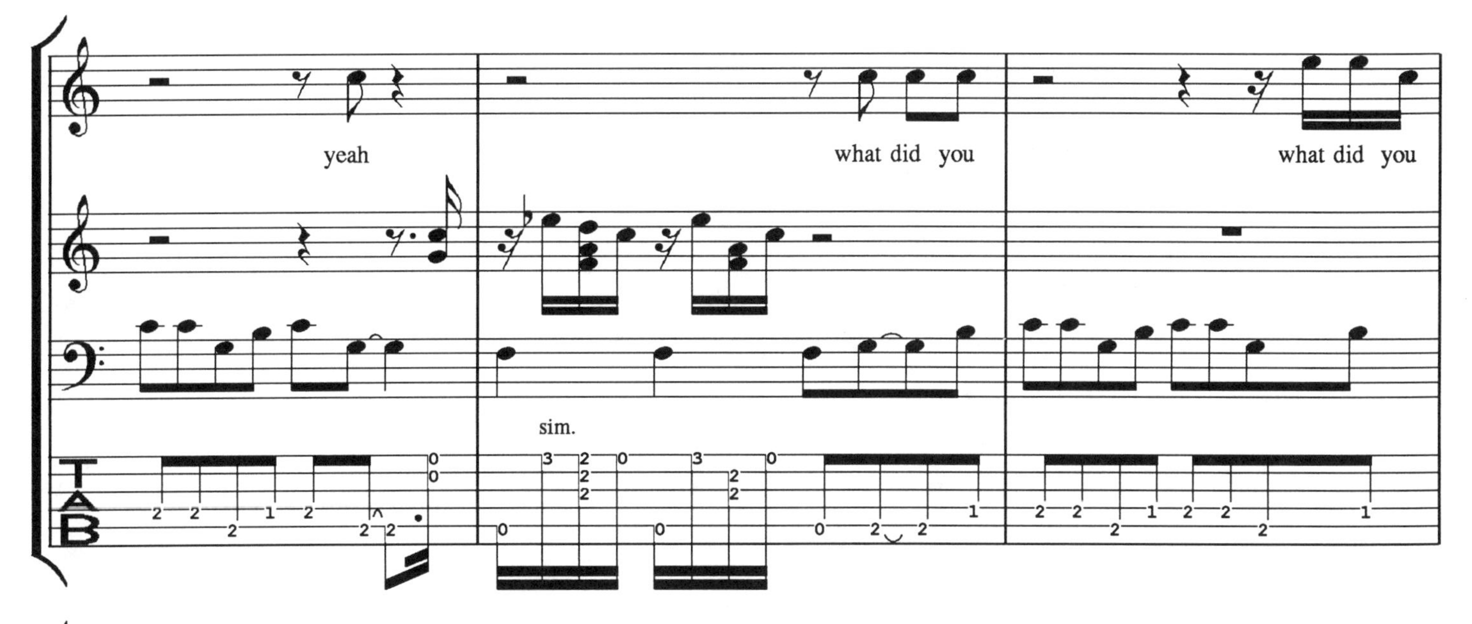
yeah
what did you
what did you
sim.

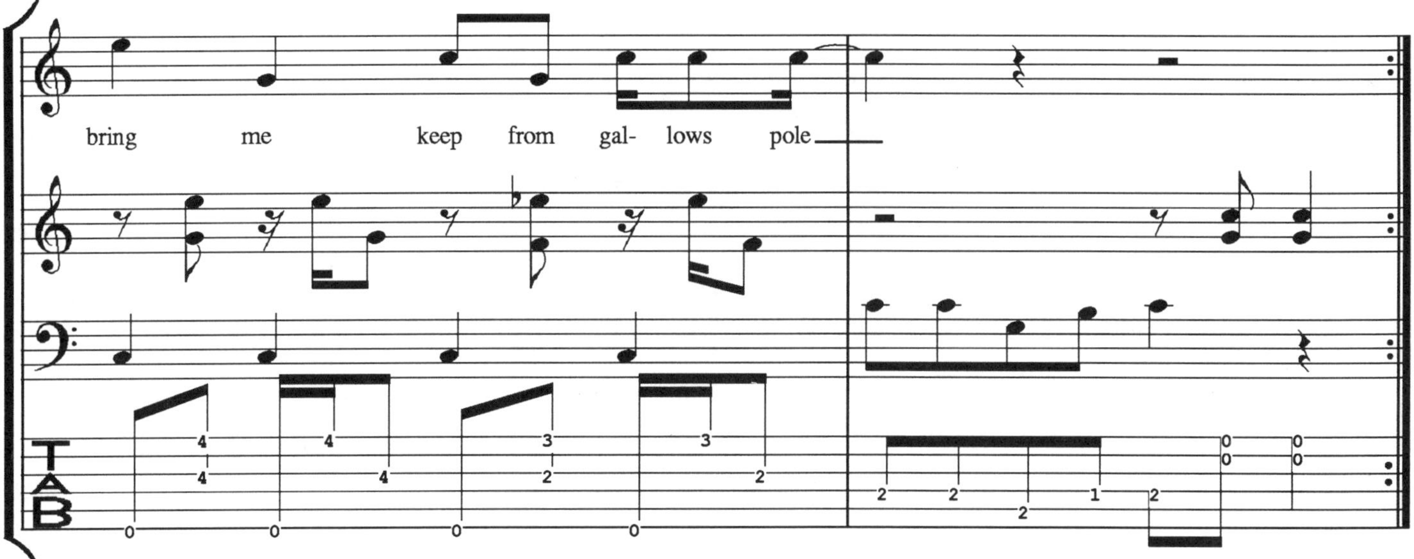
bring me keep from gal- lows pole

Fort Worth and Dallis Blues

Transcribed from 1935 American Record Company sessions released on *Leadbelly/King of the 12-String Guitar*, Columbia CD CK 46776. Another recording: *Lead Belly/The Titanic* (1935 Library of Congress sessions), Rounder CD 1097.

Lead Belly remembers that "Fort Worth and Dallis Blues" was especially popular at the Big Four Negro Resort near the Dallas terminal. ...*"Me and Blind Lemon would play that song and the women would come a-runnin'! Lawd have mercy! They'd hug and kiss us so, we could hardly play."*

Got the Fort Worth blues and the Dallis heart disease (2)
Can't keep my woman from all time worrying me.

Look here, pretty mama, tell me where you gone.
If you can't tell me, sure gonna be your wrong.

I taken you, woman, honey, to be my friend.
Yes, look what a hole, gal, you got me in.

Got the Fort Worth blues and the Dallis heart disease,
And the blues I've got, they keep on worrying me.

Good morning blues, blues how do you do?
I'm doing fairly well, baby, how are you?

You want me, baby, to be like Jesse James.

(verses from Library of Congress recording)
Got the Fort Worth blues and the Dallis heart disease.
Can't keep my woman, Lord, from worrying me.

Can't lay down for dreaming, I just can't sleep for crying.
I just can't wear that black woman off-a my mind.

If I don't go crazy, hon', I'll go stone blind
'Cause that black woman she sure do worry my mind.

The first time I met her she's holding out her hand.
When I give her my money, she gives it to her brand new man.

Got the Fort Worth blues and Dallis heart disease.
I can't help from thinking, "Do that woman love me?"

Baby, I'm so glad, hon', that I can't see.
Oh, you can't make no fat mouth outta me.

If you want me, woman, to be like Jesse James,
Take two or three shooters and rob some passenger train.

If you want me, woman, to shoot like Jesse James,
Got to pack your suitcase and find you a brand new man.

Fort Worth and Dallis Blues

Huddie Ledbetter

edited by John A. Lomax and Alan Lomax

Tempo: 125-130

Tuning: B, E, A, D, F#, B

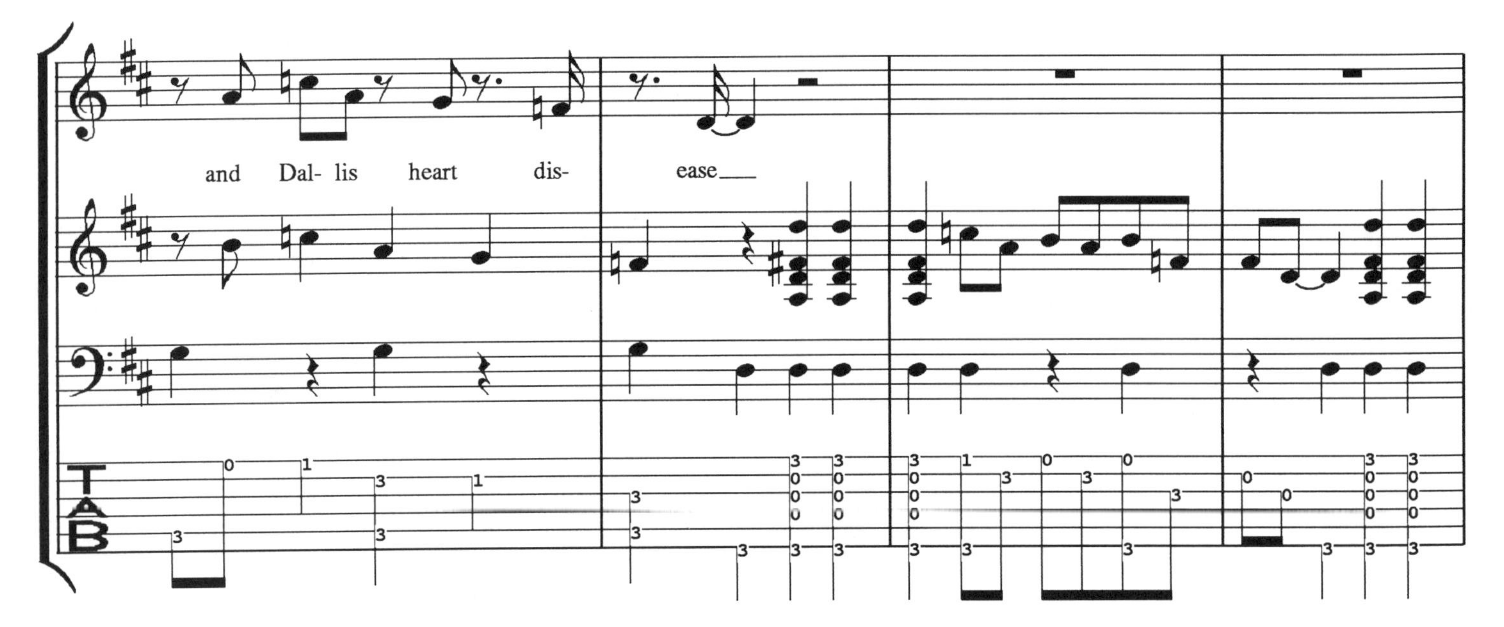
and Dal- lis heart dis-
ease___

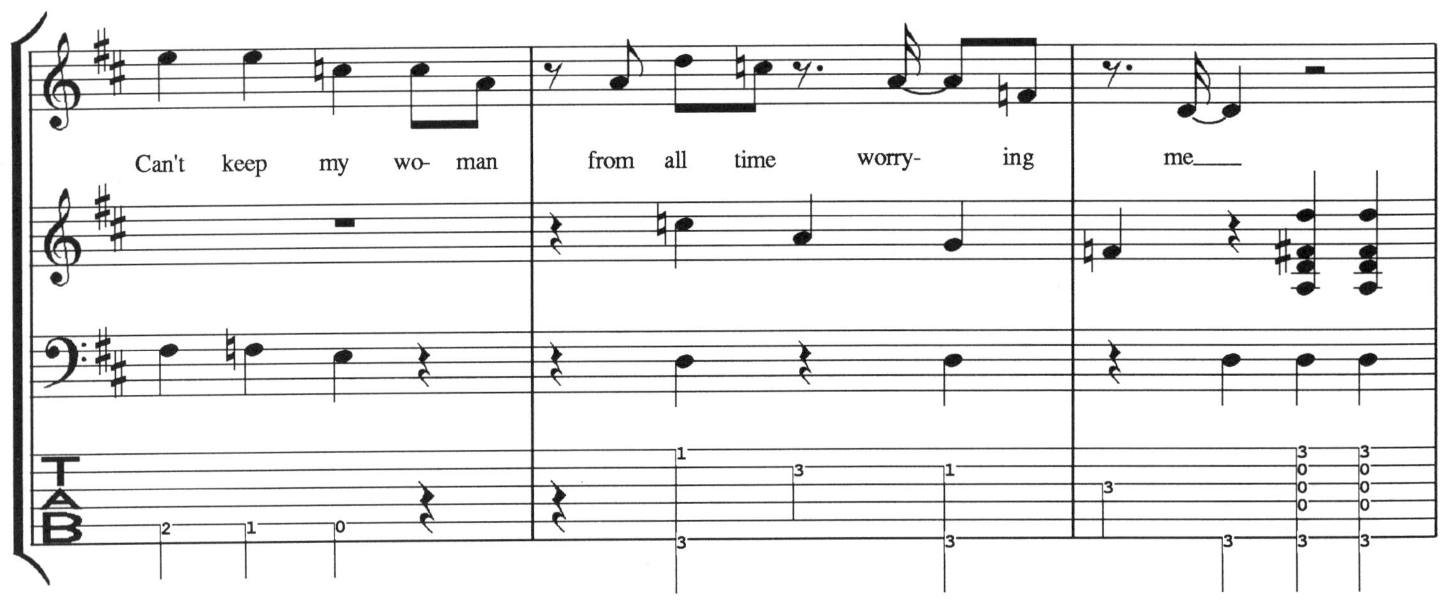
Can't keep my wo- man
from all time worry- ing
me___

1.
2.

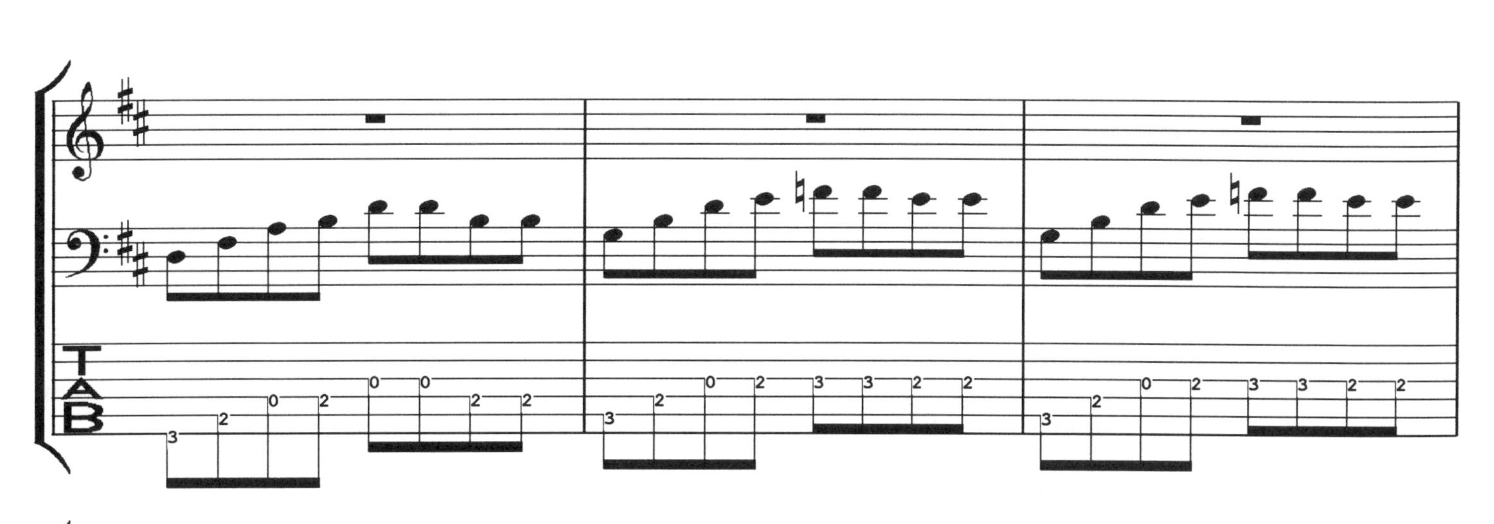

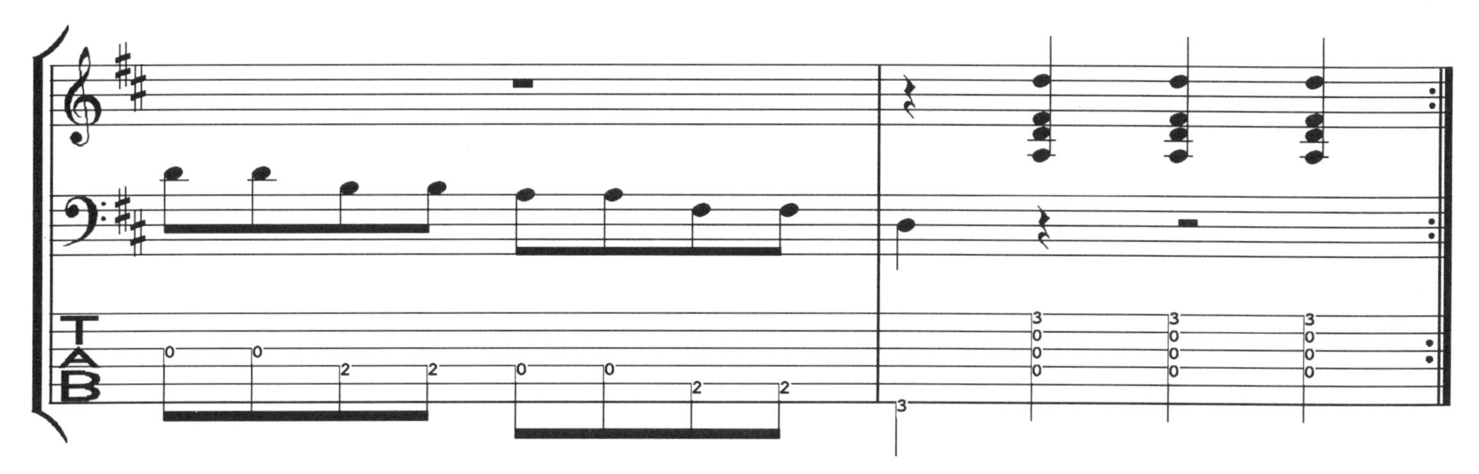

Easy Rider

Transcribed from *Lead Belly's Last Sessions* (1948), Smithsonian Folkways CD boxed set 40068/71. Other Lead Belly recordings: *Leadbelly/Alabama Bound* (1940), RCA CD 9600-2-R, *Lead Belly/Bourgeois Blues* (1944), Smithsonian Folkways CD 40045.

"Easy Rider" is a variation of the blues "C.C. Rider" available on the following Lead Belly CDs: *Leadbelly* (1935 ARC unissued sessions), Columbia 30035, *Lead Belly/Gwine Dig A Hole To Put The Devil In* (1935 Library of Congress sessions), Rounder 1045.

Easy rider, see what you done done (2)
You made me love you, now your man done come.
And it's hey, hey, hey, hey.

If you catch me stealin', please don't tell on me (2)
I'm stealin' back to my old time used-to-be.
And it's hey, hey, hey, hey.

If I was a catfish swimmin' in the deep blue sea (2)
I would start all you women divin' after me.
And it's ooh, ooh, ooh, ooh.

Easy rider, hear me callin' you,
Ooh, hear me callin' you.
Know you're three times seven, know just what you want to do.
And it's ooh, ooh, ooh, ooh.

(additional verse from RCA recording)
Every time I would see you, you was holding out your hand, baby,
Every time I would see you holding out your hand (2)
And it's hey, hey, hey, hey.

"C.C. Rider" verses:

(Columbia recording)
C.C. Rider, see what you done done.

I was lookin' right at her when that sun went down.

She was standin' in the kitchen in her mornin' gown.

Let me be your sidetrack, 'til your main line come.

(Rounder recording)
When you see me comin', put your man outdoors.

I walked up to the nation and the territo'.

I tried to find honey girl I know.

Look here, pretty mama, what you got on your mind?

Tryin' to rule, tryin' to fool that man o' mine.

Easy Rider

Huddie Ledbetter

edited by John A. Lomax and Alan Lomax

Tempo: 115-135

Tuning: B, E, A, D, F#, B

Ea- sy ri- der__ see what you done done________

ea- sy ri- der see what you done done______

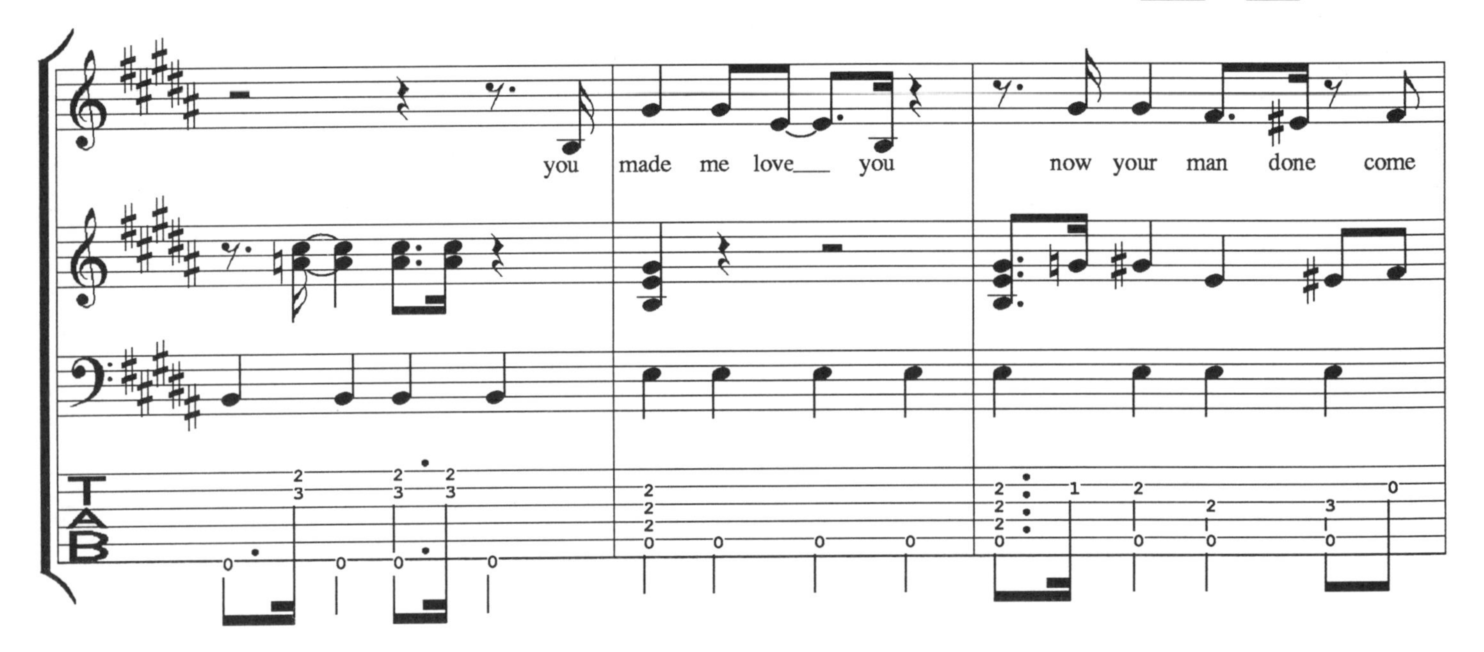
you made me love__ you now your man done come

and it's hey
T
A
B

hey hey hey
Fine
If you
T
A
B

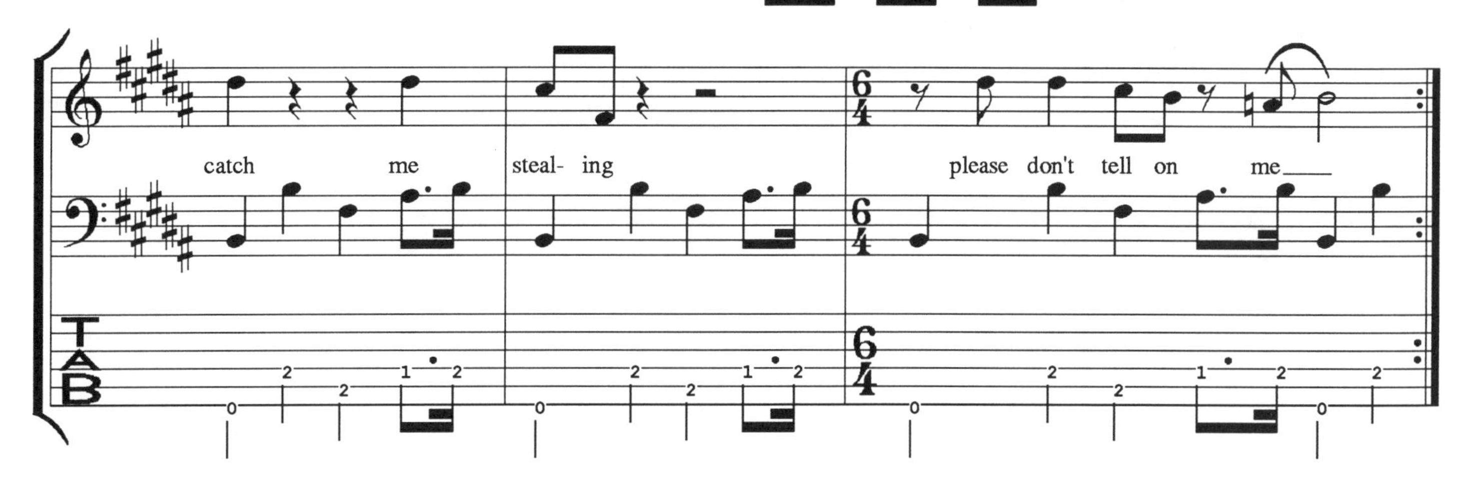
catch me steal- ing please don't tell on me
T
A
B

Big Fat Woman

Transcribed from 1943 Disc sessions originally issued in a 78 rpm album *Negro Folk Songs as Sung by Leadbelly*. This recording is currently available on the following CDs: *Lead Belly/ Where Did You Sleep Last Night?*, Smithsonian Folkways 40044; *Lead Belly/In the Shadow of the Gallows Pole*, Tradition 1018; *Leadbelly/Bourgeois Blues*, Collectables 5183.

According to Alan Lomax's liner notes for a 1950 Folkways Records reissue, Lead Belly played on the studio piano "boogie-blues the way he played them down home in Louisiana 'before all that Kansas City stuff was ever heard of.'"

Oh, Lord, big fat woman with the meat shaking on her bones.
She was born and raised in old Kentucky home.

I love my woman, tell the world I do (3)
Oh, she's so good to me, just like I to you.

I woke up this mornin' and I found my baby gone.
I was so mistreated but I wouldn't let on.

Photograph: Caufield & Shook Collection, UofL Archives

Big Fat Woman

Huddie Ledbetter

Tempo: 100-105

For piano

love my wo- man tell the world I do
I
love my wo- man tell the world I do
oh Lord I love
my wo- man tell the world I do
oh she's
so good to me just like I to
you
I

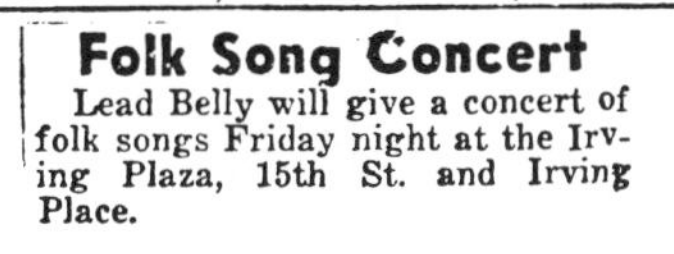
DAILY NEWS, THURSDAY, MAY 15, 1947

Folk Song Concert

Lead Belly will give a concert of folk songs Friday night at the Irving Plaza, 15th St. and Irving Place.

You Know I Got To Do It

Transcribed from *Lead Belly's Last Sessions* (1948) now available on Smithsonian Folkways CD set 40068/71 under the title "Well, You Know I Had To Do It." A much shorter recording of the song also appears on the same CD set.

Chorus:
Well, you know I got to do it,
Yes, you know I got to do it (2)
And I can't bust a-loose my gal.

Mississippi River so deep and wide,
I can't get a letter from the other side. (Chorus)

I jumped in the river, I started to drown,
I thought about my woman and I turned around
You know I had to do it (etc.)

I take her to a dance, she danced with another.
Wound up gettin' married, she swore it was her brother.
You know she had to do it (etc.)

First time I met her, I met her at a stand.
Hit me 'side the head, said, "Big boy, won't you be my man?"
You know I had to do it (etc.)

I knocked on her door about half past ten.
When I heard her cryin', said, "You can't come in."
You know she had to do it (etc.)

Lead Belly and his wife Martha, 1940s Photo: James Chapelle Lead Belly Archives

You Know I Got To Do It

Huddie Ledbetter

Tempo: 130-150

Tuning: B, E, A, D, F#, B

and I can't bust- a loose my gal
Pull off

Mis- sis- sip- pi Riv- er so deep and wide I can't get a let- ter

from the oth- er side well you know I got to do it yes

you know I got to do it
yes you know I got to do it

and I can't bust- a loose
that gal
Pull off

Silver City Bound

Transcribed from *Lead Belly's Last Sessions* (1948), Smithsonian Folkways boxed CD set 40068/71. Elements from the same song also appear on the track "Blind Lemon" on *Lead Belly/ Where Did You Sleep Last Night?*, Smithsonian Folkways CD 40044.

Silver City was a suburb of Dallas. Lead Belly and his buddy Blind Lemon Jefferson would perform on board the interurban bus.

Silver City bound, I'm Silver City bound.
Well, I tell my baby, I'm Silver City bound.
Me and Blind Lemon gonna ride on down. (2)
Catch me by the hand, oh baby.
Blind Lemon was a blind man
Catch me by the hand, oh baby,
And lead me all through the land.

Lead Belly Archives

Silver City Bound

Huddie Ledbetter

edited by Alan Lomax

Tempo: 115-145

Tuning: C, F, A#, D#, G, C

ba- by
I'm Sil- ver Cit- y bound

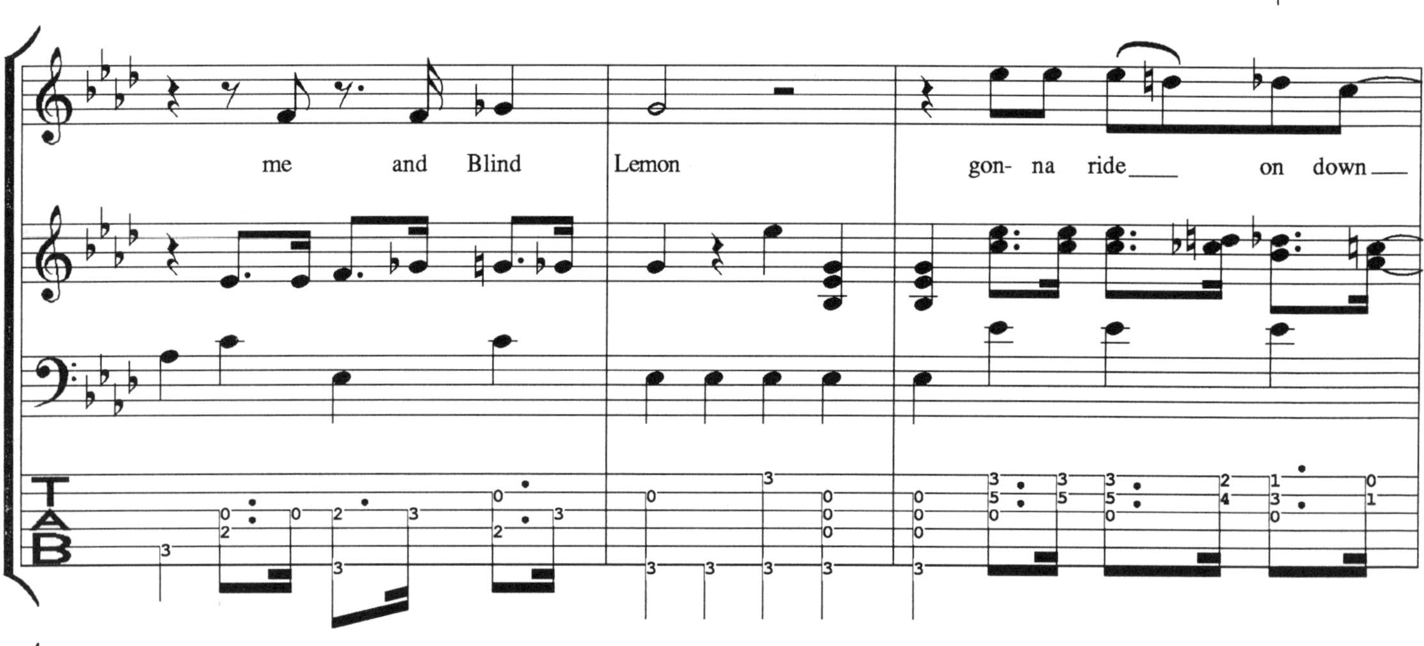
me and Blind Lemon
gon- na ride on down

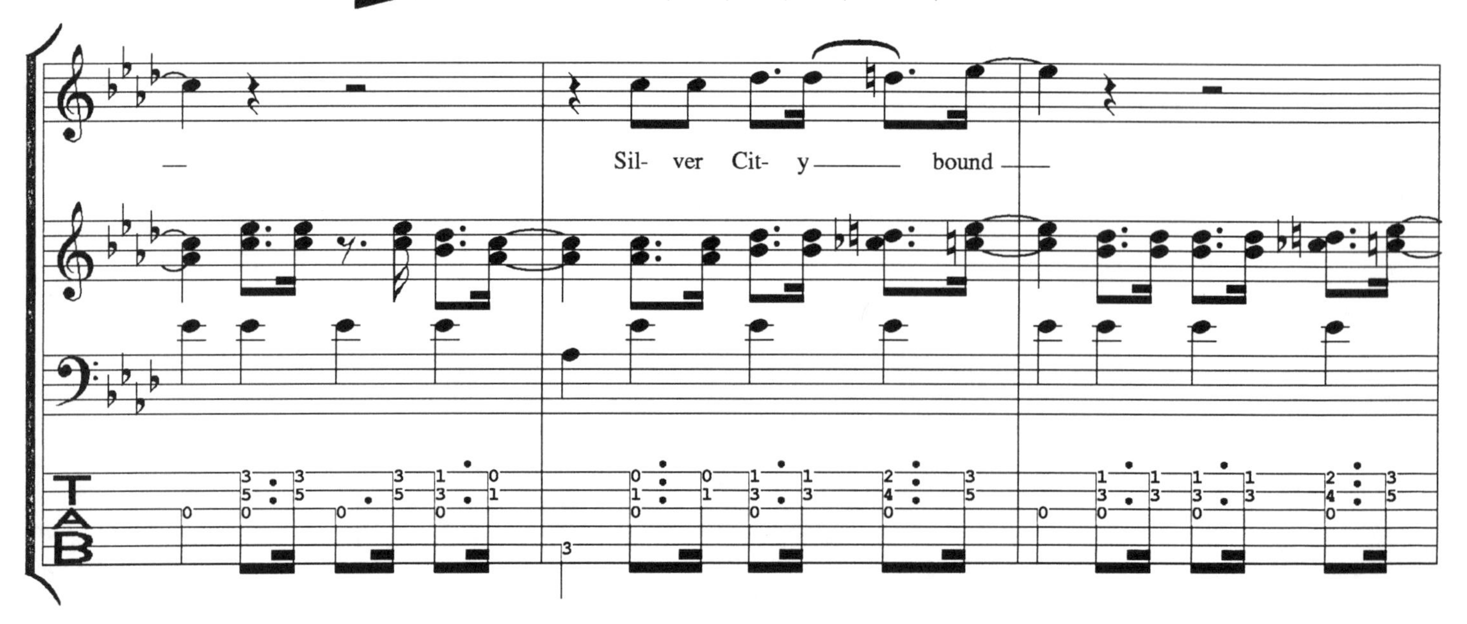
Sil- ver Cit- y bound

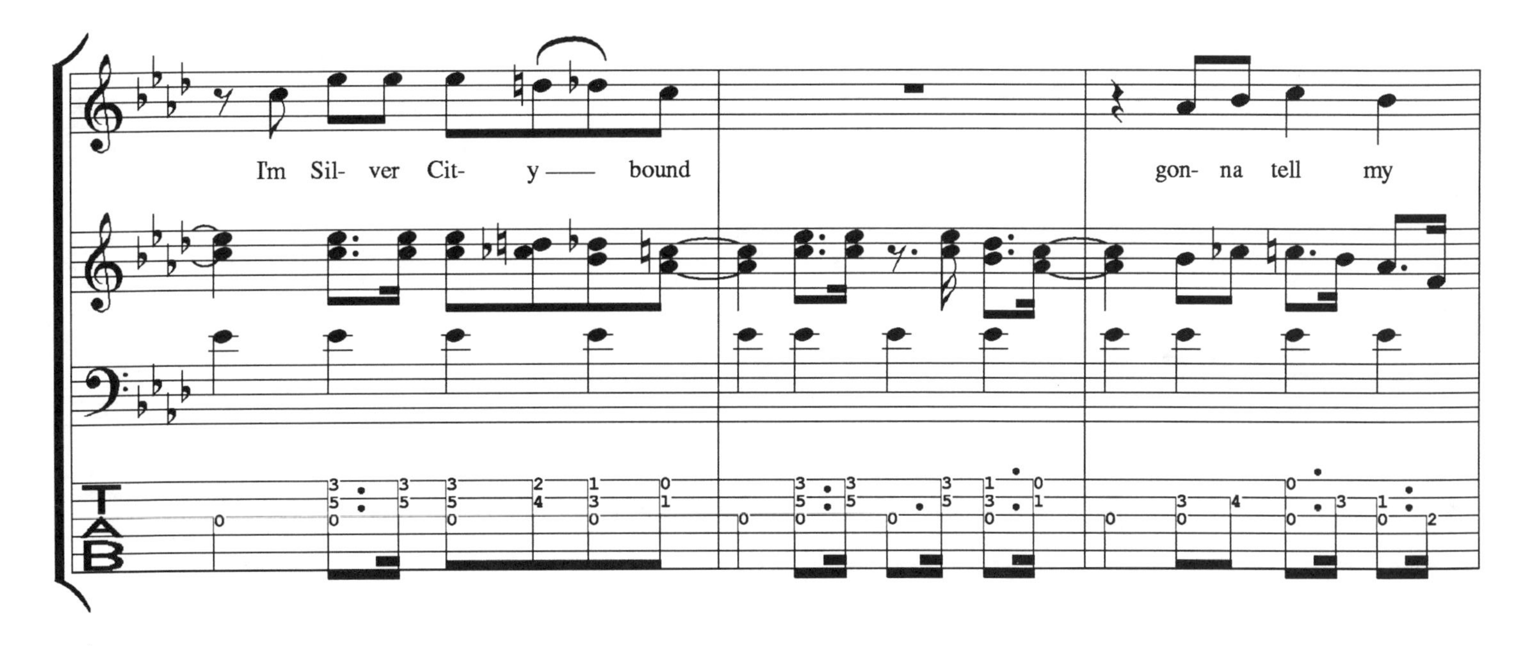
I'm Sil- ver Cit- y — bound
gon- na tell my

ba- by
Sil- ver Cit- y bound

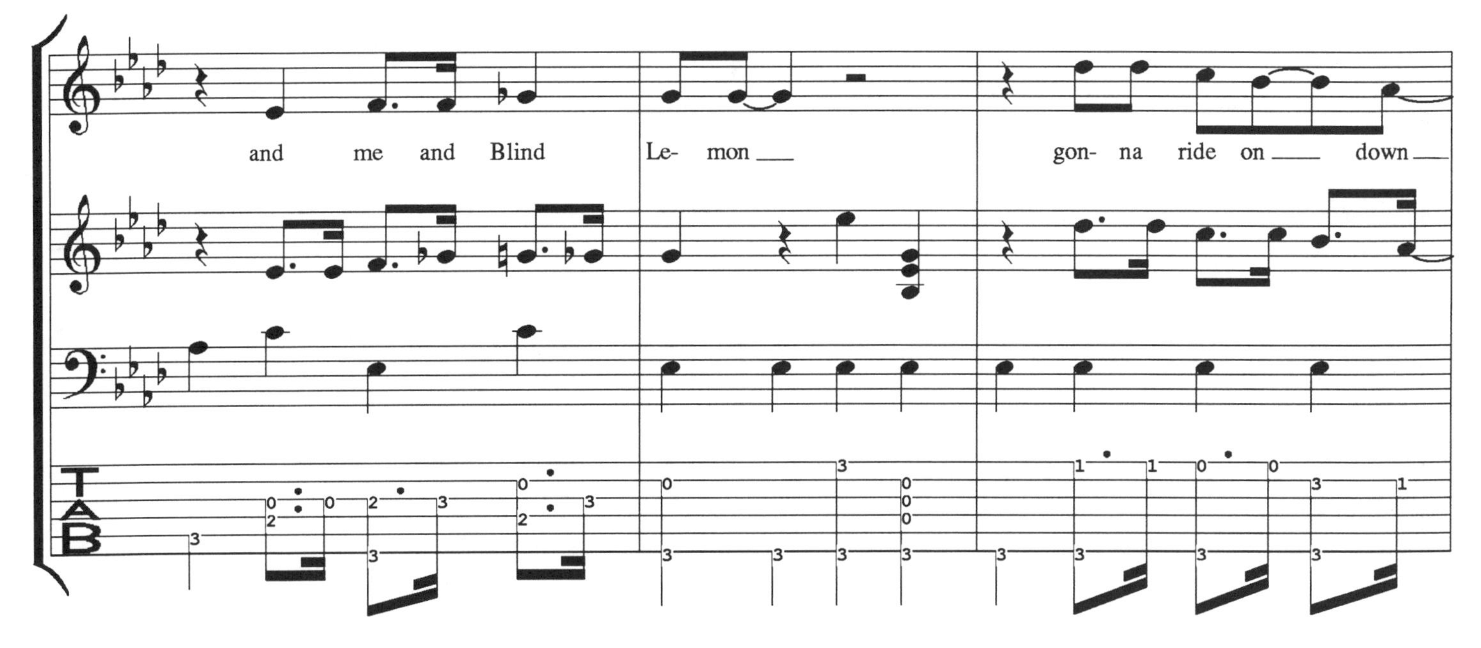
and me and Blind
Le- mon
gon- na ride on down

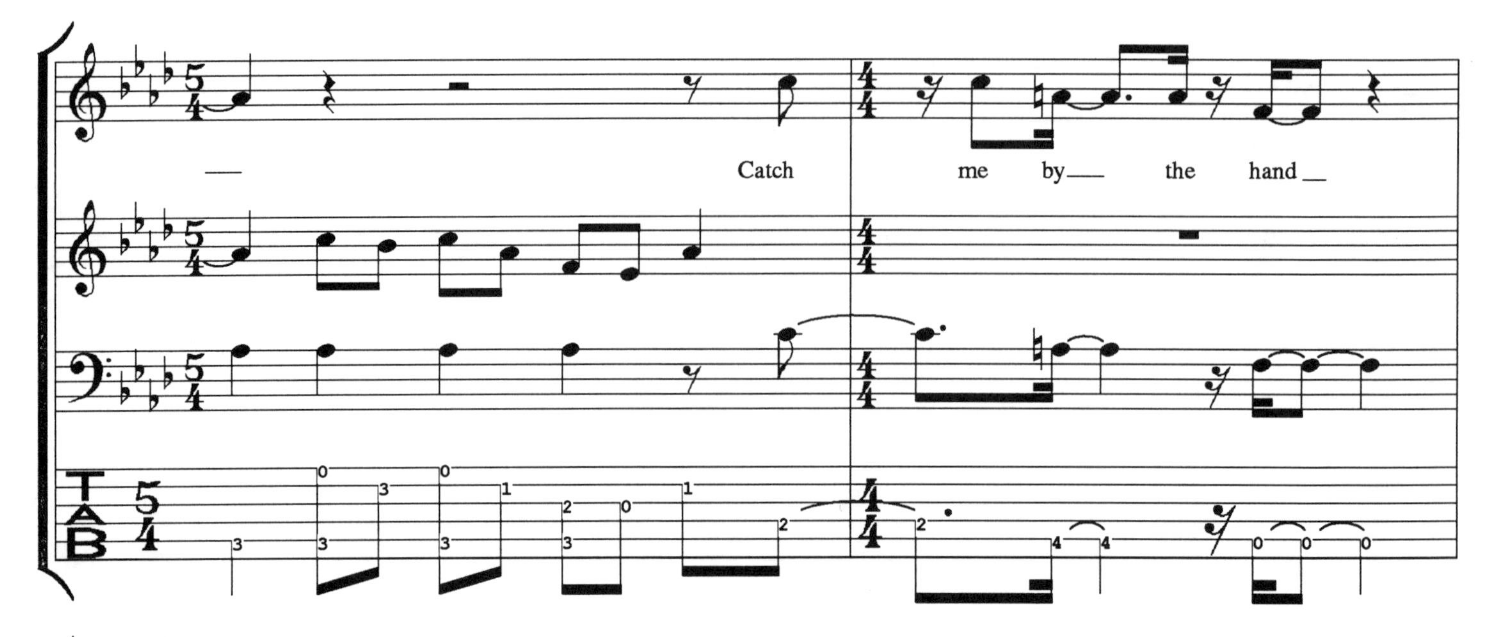
Catch
me by the hand

oh ba-
by

Blind Le-
mon was a blind man
Catch

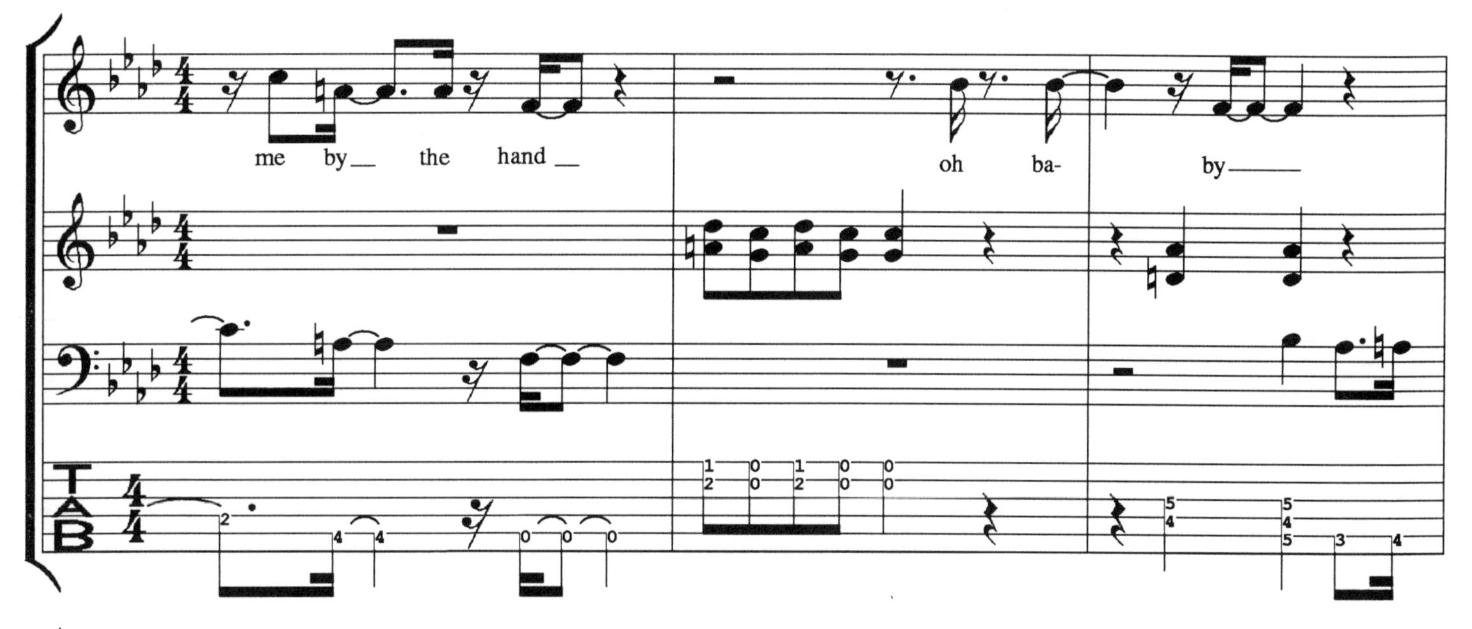
me by__ the hand __
oh ba-
by______

and lead me all through the land ________

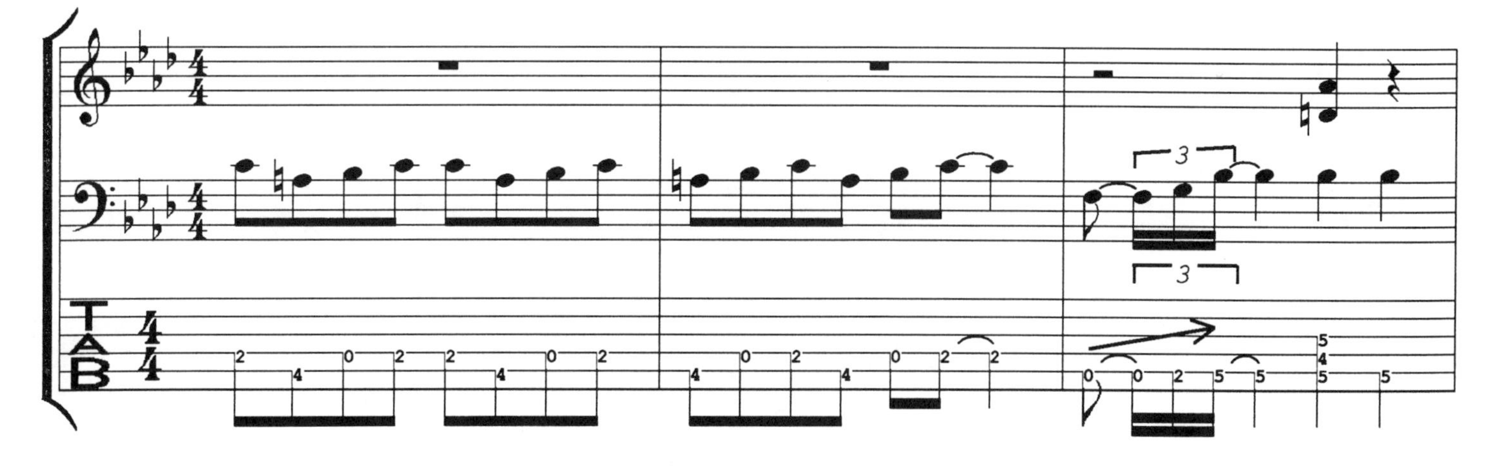

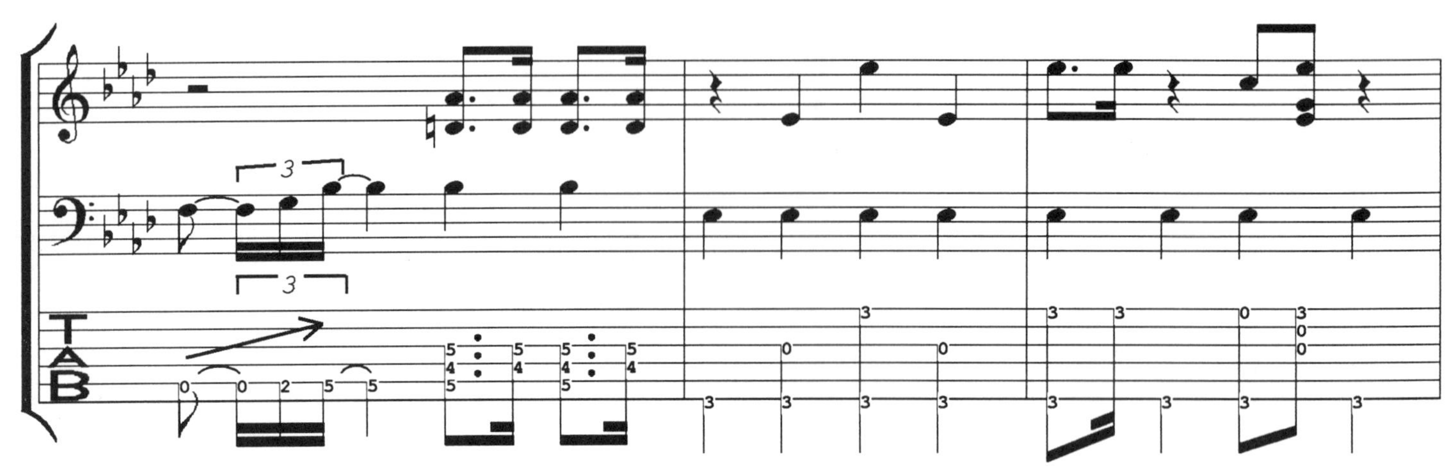

sim.
sim.

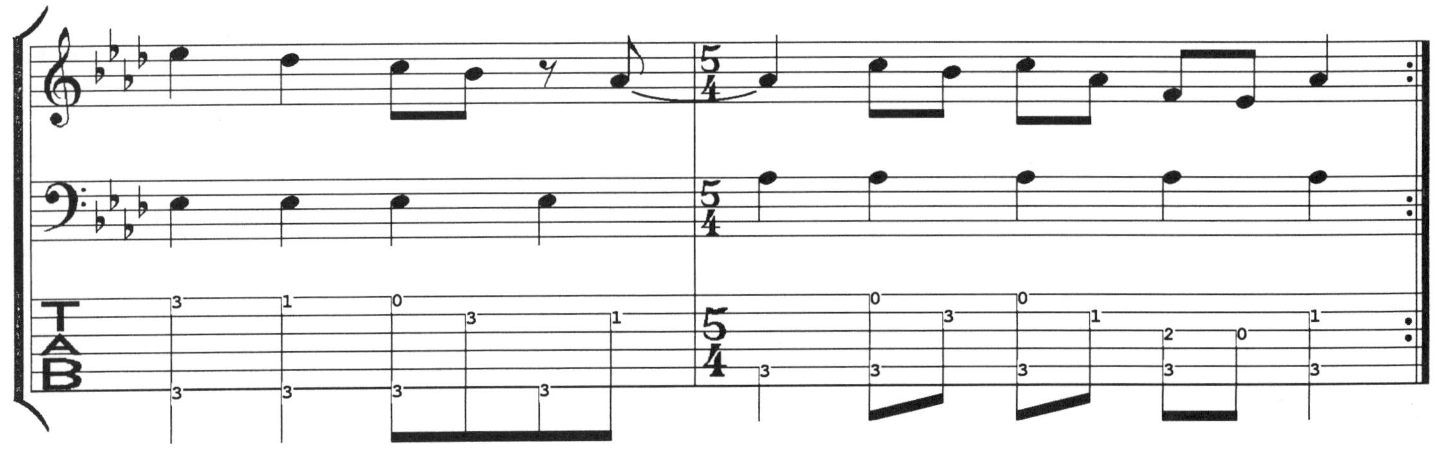

Bourgeois Blues

Transcribed from 1938 Library of Congress sessions now available on *Lead Belly/Gwine Dig a Hole to Put the Devil In*, Rounder CD 1045. Other CD recordings: *Lead Belly/In the Shadow of the Gallows Pole*, Tradition 1018, *Leadbelly/Bourgeois Blues* and *Lead Belly Memorial Vols. 3 & 4*, Collectables 5183 and 5604 (1939 Musicraft sessions);*Lead Belly/Bourgeois Blues*, Smithsonian Folkways 40045 and *Mean Old World/The Blues from 1940 to 1944*, Smithsonian Collection of Recordings – one track of a 4 CD boxed set RD 110 MSD4-35974 (1944 Folkways sessions).

Recordings by other musicians: Ry Cooder, Arlo Guthrie, Pete Seeger, Taj Mahal.

The powerful social statement in this song developed from an incident in Washington, D.C. in which Lead Belly's interracial party was denied entrance to both white and black facilities. Martha is his wife, and Miss Barnicle is a white New York college professor and friend who had Lead Belly sing for her students.

Chorus:
Oh, he's a bourgeois man
Living in a bourgeois town.
I got the bourgeois blues,
And I'm sure gonna spread the news.

Me and Miss Barnicle went all over town;
I heard a colored man say, "You can't come around." *(Chorus)*

Me and Martha were standin' upstairs;
I heard a white man say, "I don't want no niggers up there." *(Chorus)*

I'm gonna tell all the colored people, I want 'em to understand;
Washington ain't no place for no colored man.
'Cause it's a bourgeois town, *(etc.)*

The white folks in Washington, they know how
To chuck you a nickel just to see a nigger bow.
'Cause it's a bourgeois town, *(etc.)*

I got something to tell you just before I go,
I want everybody to know.
'Cause it's a bourgeois town, *(etc.)*

I want all the colored people to listen to me,
Don't ever try to get no home in Washington, D.C.
'Cause it's a bourgeois town, *(etc.)*

(alternate verses)
Me and my wife run all over town,
Everywhere we go the people would turn us down.

Home of the brave, land of the free,
I don't wanna be mistreated by no bourgeoisie.

(alternate chorus)
Lord, it's a bourgeois town.
Whee, it's a bourgeois town.
I got the bourgeois blues.
I'm gonna spread the news all around.

Bourgeois Blues

Huddie Ledbetter

edited by Alan Lomax

Tempo: 105-120
Tuning: B, E, A, D, F#, B

I got the bour- geois blues and I'm sure gon- na spread the news

Me and Miss Bar- ni-

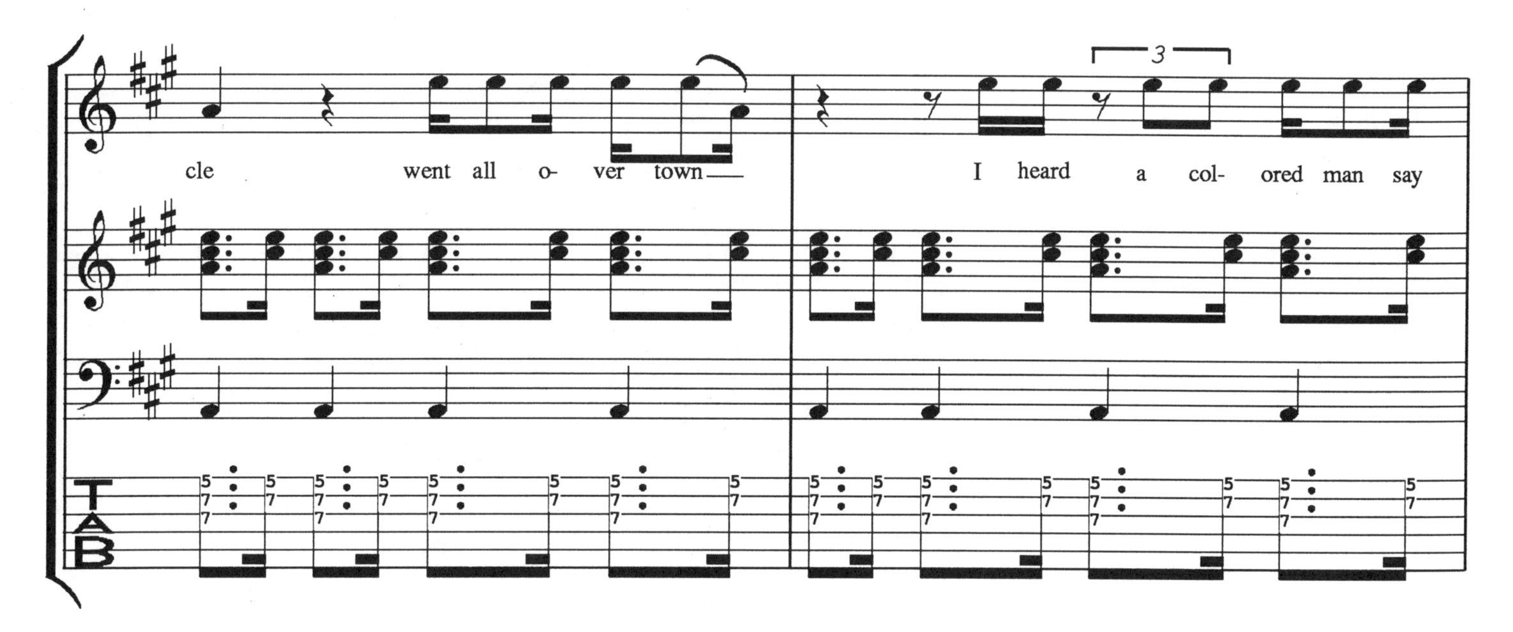
cle went all o- ver town
I heard a col- ored man say

you can't come a- round he's a bour- geois man

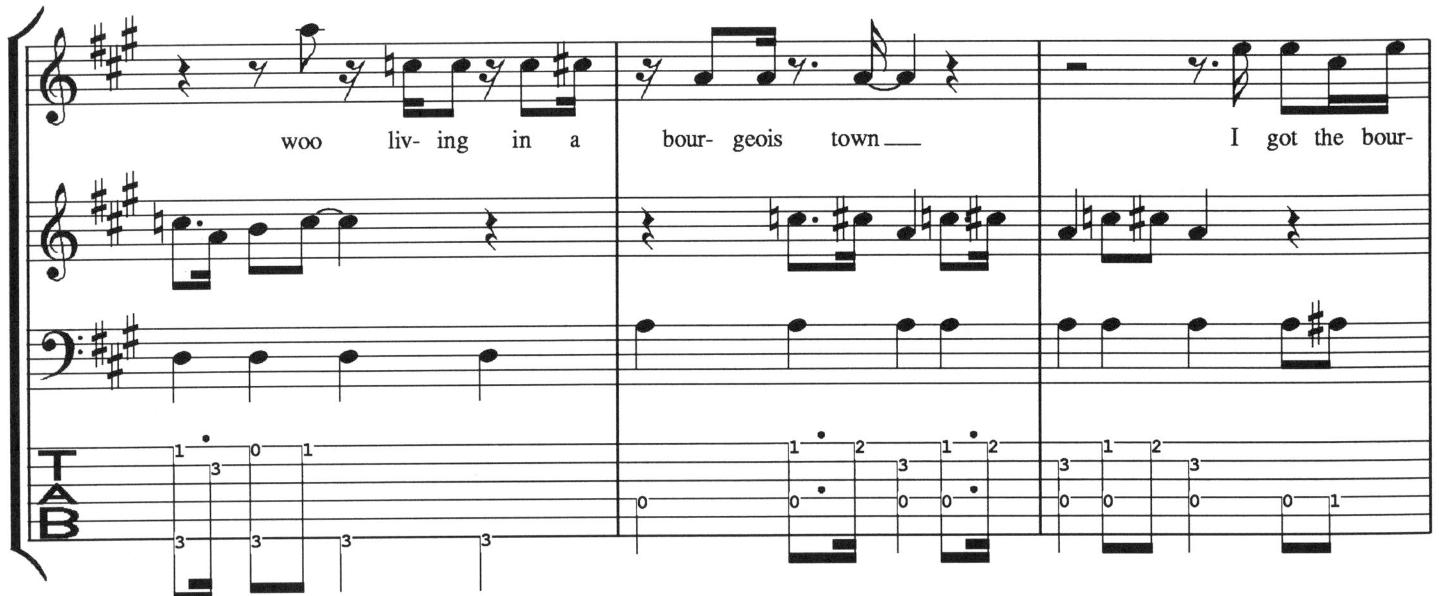
woo liv- ing in a bour- geois town I got the bour-

geois blues and I'm sure gon- na spread the news

De Kalb Blues

Transcribed from 1939 Musicraft recording sessions now available on the following CDs: *Leadbelly/Bourgeois Blues* and *Lead Belly Memorial Vols. 3 & 4*, Collectables 5183 and 5604, *Lead Belly/In the Shadow of the Gallows Pole*, Tradition 1018. Another Lead Belly recording: *Lead Belly/Midnight Special* (1935 Library of Congress sessions), Rounder CD 1044.

Lead Belly received a thirty-year prison sentence while living near De Kalb, Texas.

De Kalb blues, Lord, make me feel so bad,
Just to think about the times I once have had.

Wasn't for the powder and the straightenin' comb,
Lord, the De Kalb women would not have no home.

Blues was whiskey, I would stay drunk all the time,
I'd stay drunk, baby, to wear you off my mind.

De Kalb blues, Lord, make me feel so bad,
Just to think about the times I once have had.

Feel like walkin', feel like stoppin' here,
Like to find some woman, baby, to feel my care.

Look here, woman, see what you done done,
You made me love you, now your man done come.

(additional verses from 1935 recording)
Wasn't for the powder and the store bought hair,
Then De Kalb women would not go nowhere.

Buy me a pistol, get me a Gatlin' gun
If I carried you baby, we gonna have some fun.

Some folks told me De Kalb blues wasn't bad,
Why them's the worstest blues that I ever had.

Look here, baby, see what you told me,
I'm down in mind and worried, everything I see.

Feelin', baby, jump overboard and drown,
Singing about my woman, she done left this town.

Jumped in the river and I started to drown,
Thought about my baby, and I turned around.

Look here, baby, what more can I do?
Lord, I had five dollars, then I'd give you two.

Some folks told me De Kalb blues wasn't bad,
I done give you, baby, all the money I had.

(Additional verses as printed in
"Negro Folk Songs As Sung By Lead Belly")
Won't cook no dinner, won't wash no clothes,
Woman, you won't do nothin', hon', but walk the road.

Heart ain't iron, babe, must be marble stone,
'Cause I took you in when you did not have no home.

Good-lookin' woman, can I go home with you?
I done ask you, that's all a poor boy can do.

Heard you had money, and I come to see,
Would you take a poor old slave like me?

You can go if you ain't feared of my man,
He's a bad man with a forty-one in his hand.

Bad man comin', comin' with his gun,
I ain't got a gun but I ain't gonna run.

I'd rather be dead and be in my grave,
Than be here to be some woman's slave.

Train I'm ridin' don't do no stoppin' here,
Keep on ridin', find some woman to feel my care.

Come here, baby, let me hold your hand,
Bet my bottom dollar, you got a brand new man.

Took you in baby, you did not have no home,
Thank God I leaved you, baby, and that's all.

First time I met you, cryin' for a nickel or a dime,
When you cooked my dinner, you swear you ain't got time.

De Kalb blues, babe, make me feel so bad,
That must have been the De Kalb blues I had.

Oh Lordy, babe, sit down on my knees,
Someone took my pistol and my B.V.D.s.

De Kalb Blues

Huddie Ledbetter

edited by John A. Lomax and Alan Lomax

Tempo: 105-140

Tuning: C,F,A#,D#,G,C

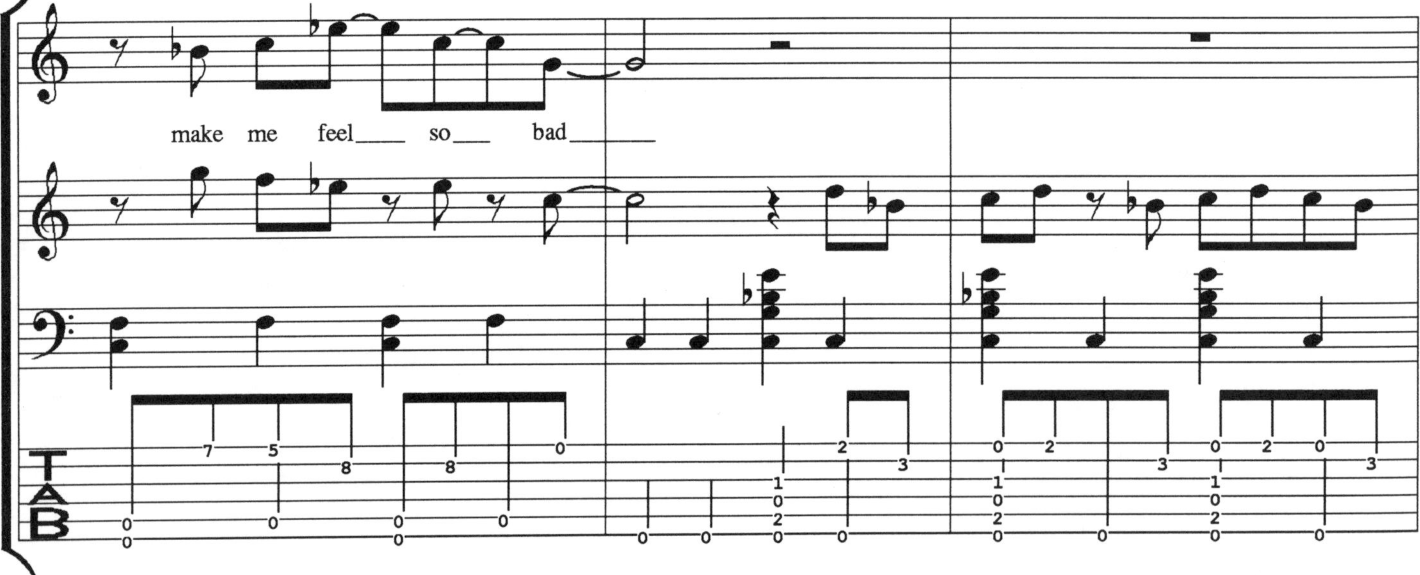

De Kalb blues
Lord
make me feel
so
bad

just to think
a-
bout

the times
I
once have had

Fannin St., 1919 Photograph courtesy LSU Shreveport, Noel Memorial Library Archives

"Lead Belly's songs were actually dramatizations of things that had gone on in his life. And when he sang, the song had something in it, a real story.

When Lead got on the stage all the emotions that came through were right out of the life he had known and lived."

Brownie McGhee

Fannin Street

(Mr. Tom Hughes' Town)

Transcribed from *Lead Belly's Last Sessions* LP boxed set (1948); the song is lower in pitch on the Smithsonian Folkways boxed CD pressing 40068/71 which includes another performance of the same song under title "Cry For Me." Other Lead Belly CD recordings: *Leadbelly* (1935 ARC sessions), Columbia CK 30035; *Lead Belly/The Titanic* (1935 Library of Congress sessions), Rounder 1097; *Lead Belly Memorial Vols. 3 & 4* (1939 Musicraft sessions), Collectables 5604; *Lead Belly/Bourgeois Blues* (undated Folkways archives), Smithsonian Folkways 40045. The title "I'm On My Last Go Round" on *Leadbelly/Alabama Bound* (1940), RCA 9600-2-R is a variant of this song.

Shreveport, Louisiana where Tom Hughes was sheriff, is the location of this song – Lead Belly's own estimate of the most important conflict of his life.

Follow me down, follow me down,
Follow me down by Mister Tom Hughes' town.

My momma told me, my little sister too,
Women on Fannin Street, son, they gonna be the death of you.

I told my momma, momma you don't know,
Women on Fannin Street kill me, why don't you let me go.

I went to my momma, fell down on my knees,
Crying, "Oh Lordy, momma, will you forgive me please?"

*I got a woman living on Stony Hill,**
Been running all over town with Buffalo Bill.

You been running all over town with Buffalo Bill,
Two chances to one, baby, you done got kill.

If anybody should ask you who compose this song,
Tell 'em Huddie Ledbetter done been here and gone.

*Stoner Hill is a neighborhood in Shreveport.
This nonsensical verse was inserted to take the place of a vulgar one.

(additional verses from RCA recording)
Follow me down (3)
I'm on my last go round.
I am broke and hungry,
Ragged and dirty too.
I just want to know, gal,
Can I go home with you?

Settin' down here wonderin'
Will a matchbox hold my clothes?
I don't want to be bothered
With no suitcase on my road.

Follow me down (3)
'Cause I'm on my last go round.

Fannin Street

(Mr. Tom Hughes' Town)

Huddie Ledbetter

edited by John A. Lomax and Alan Lomax

Tempo: 103-125

Tuning: C,F,A#,D#,G,C

wo- men on Fan- nin Street son they gon- na be the death of you
oo oo oo oo
I told my mom- ma
mom- ma you don't know
wo- men on Fan- nin Street kill me why

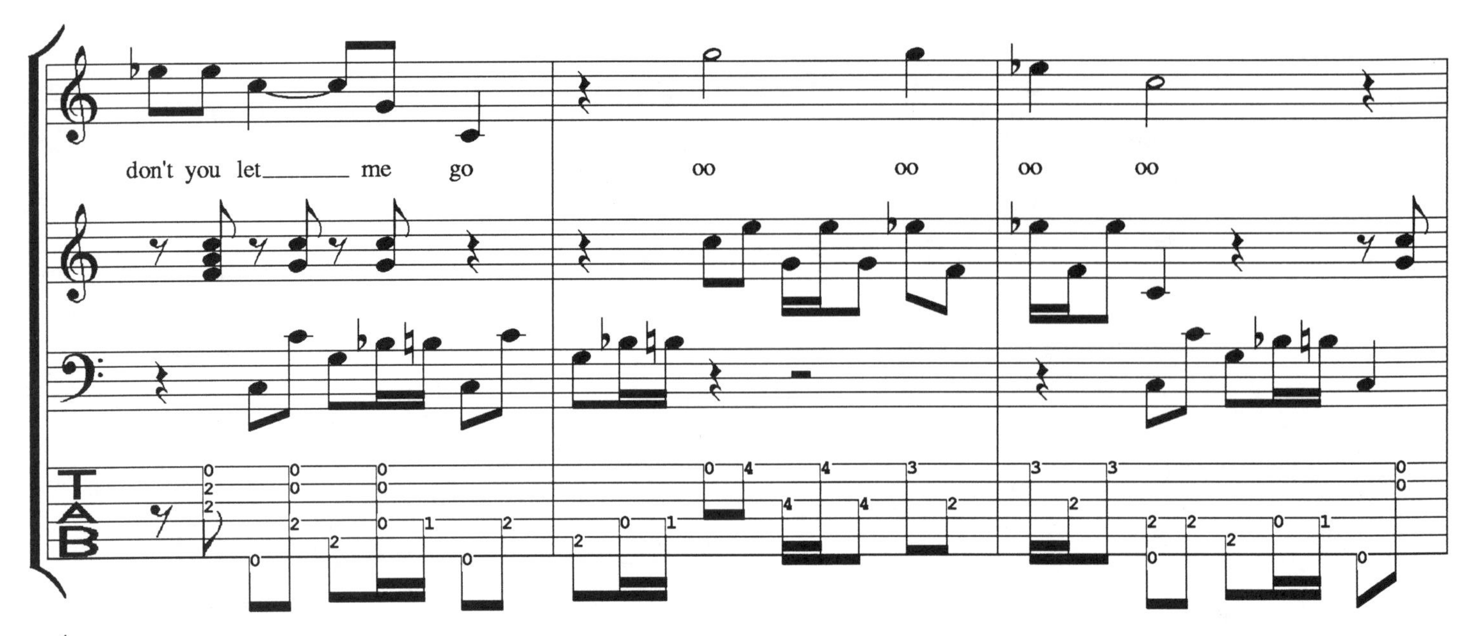
don't you let ___ me go
oo oo
oo oo
TAB

oo ___ oo ___
oo ___ oo
TAB

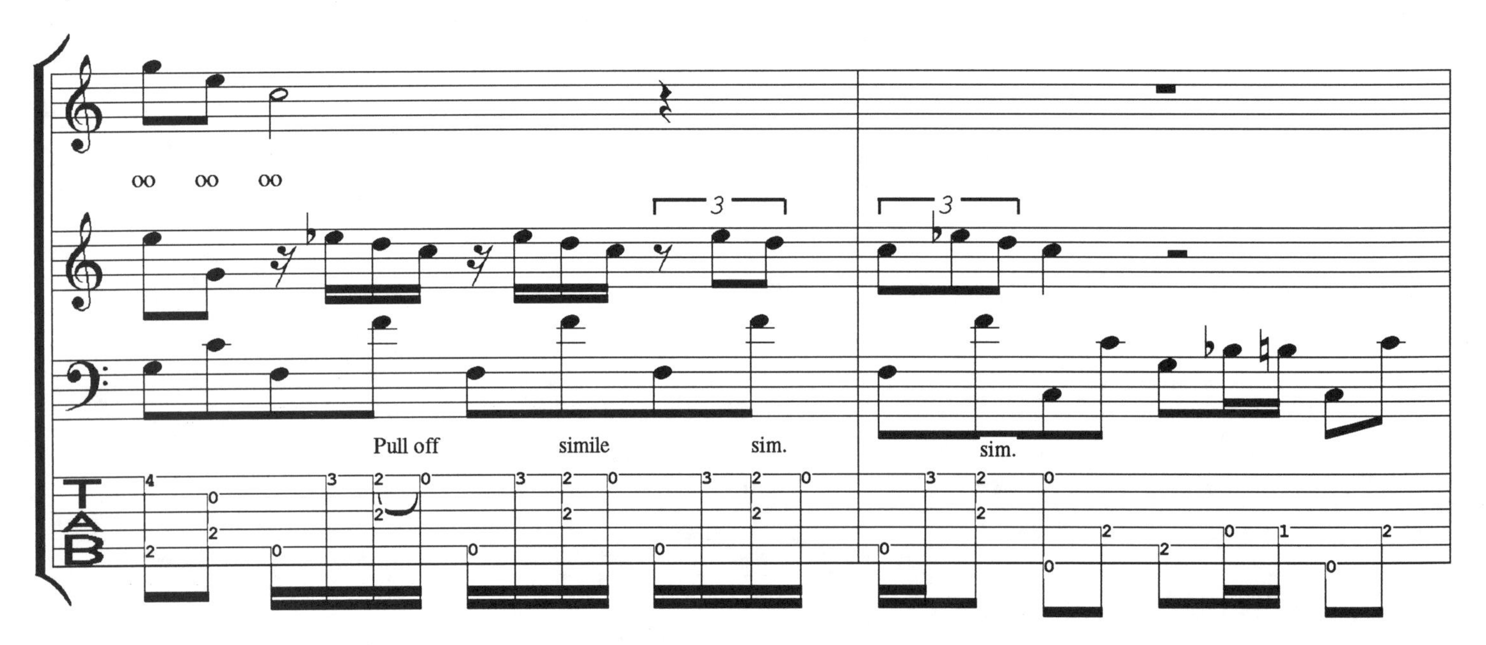
oo oo oo
Pull off
simile
sim.
sim.
TAB

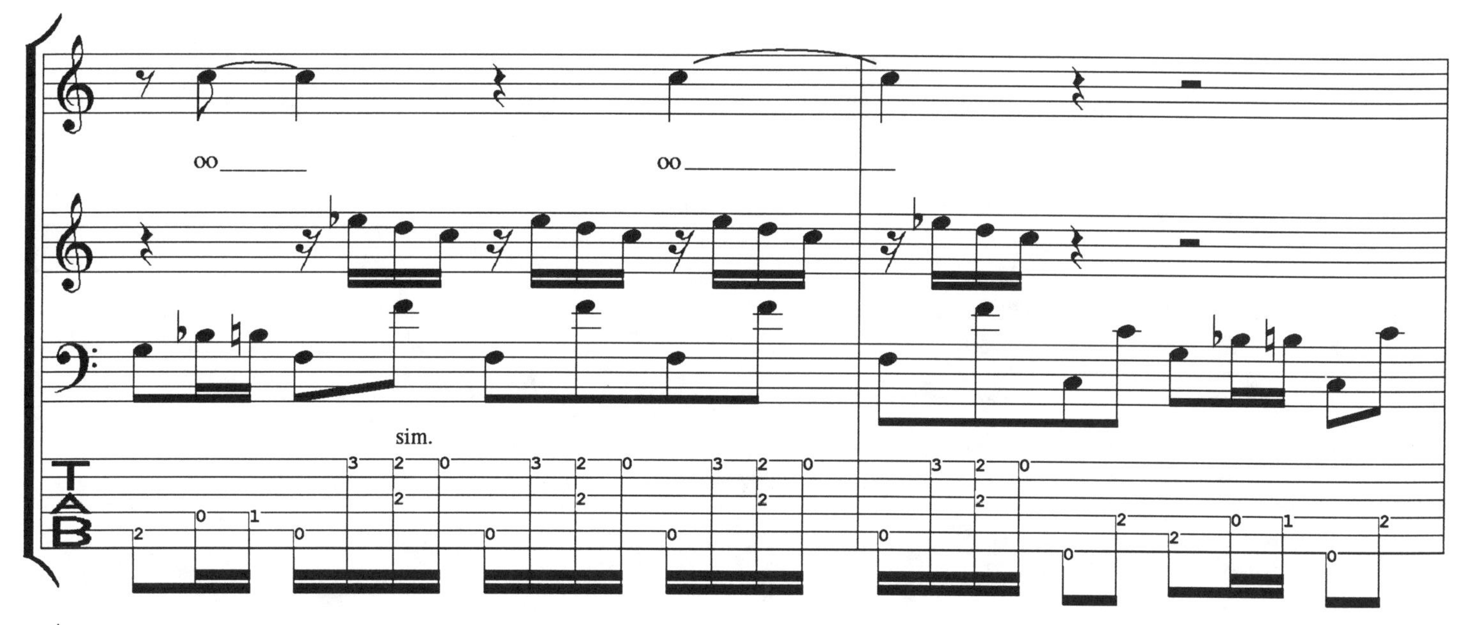
oo
oo
sim.

mm
mm
mm

sim.

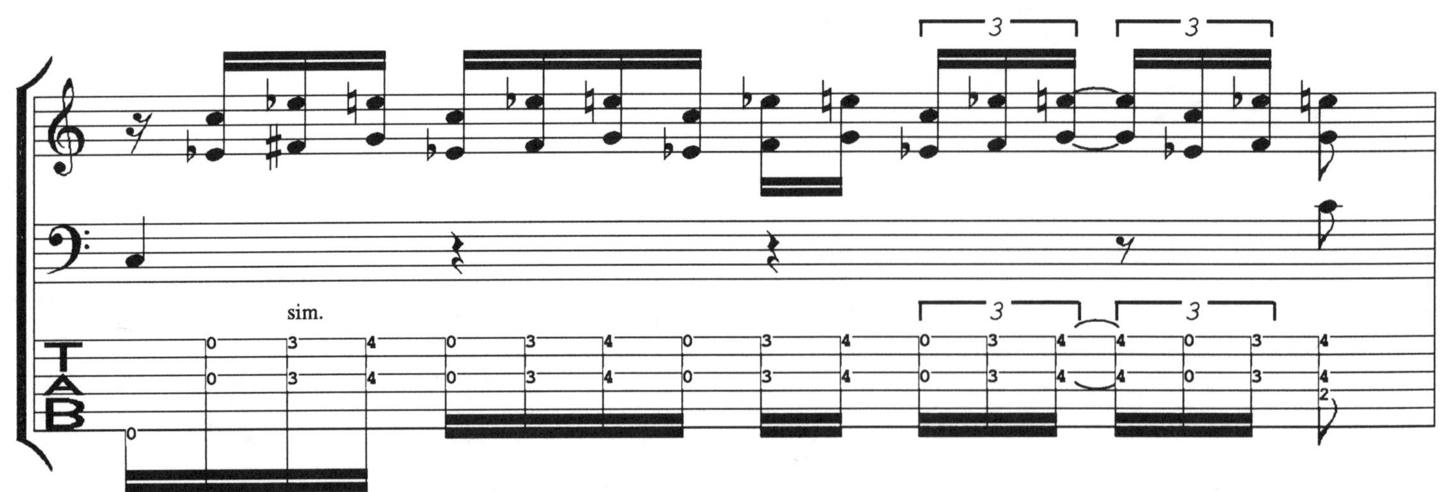
sim.

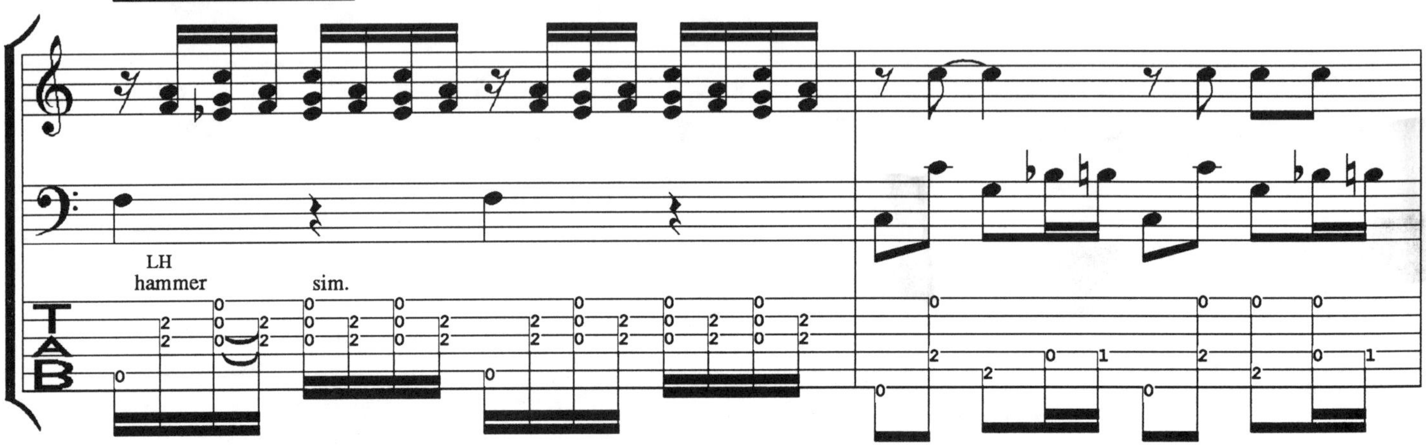
LH
hammer
sim.

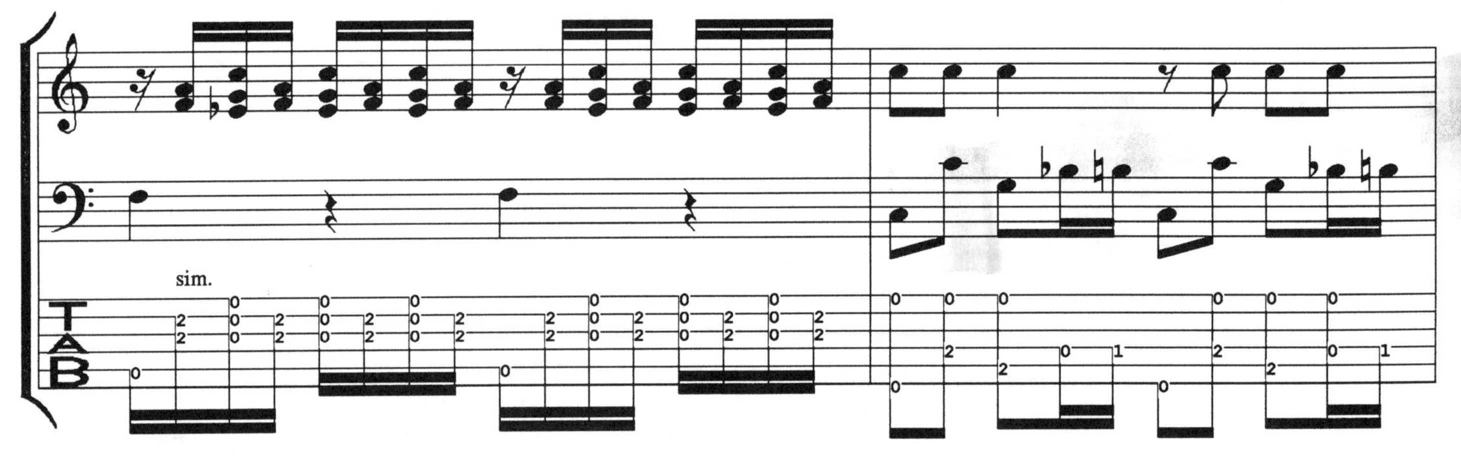
sim.

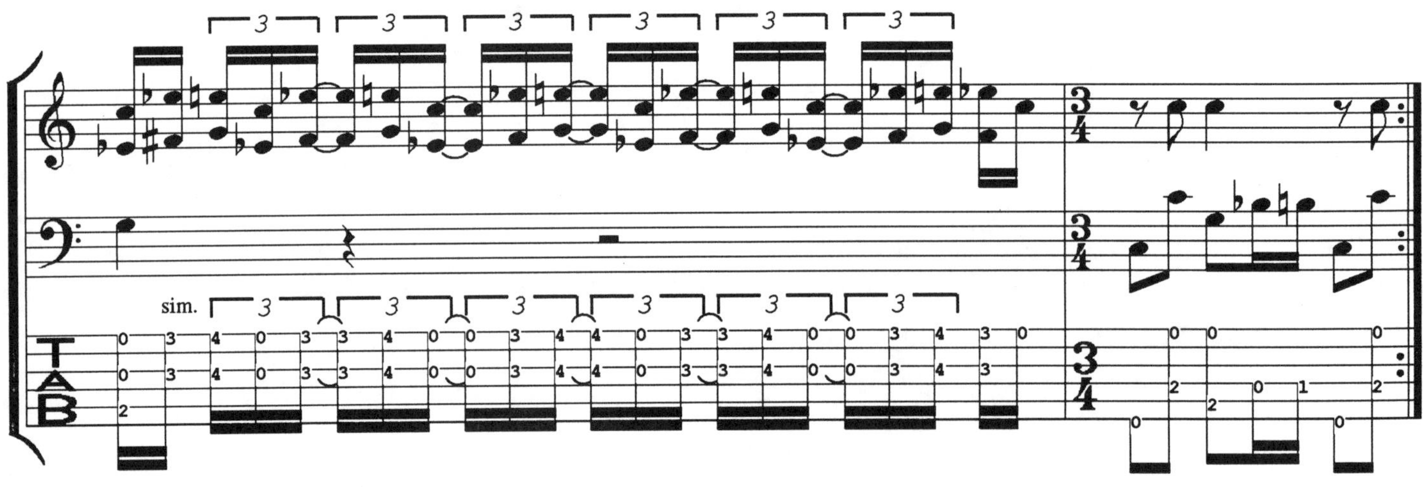
sim.

Ain't Going Down To The Well No More/Go Down, Old Hannah

Medley transcribed from April 1939 Musicraft recording sessions now available on *Lead Belly Memorial Vols. 3 & 4*, Collectables CD 5604. Other CD recordings: "Ain't Going Down" – *Lead Belly/Nobody Knows the Trouble I've Seen*, Rounder 1098; "Go Down, Old Hannah" – *Lead Belly/Go Down Old Hannah*, Rounder 1099 (1935 Library of Congress sessions); and *Lead Belly's Last Sessions* (1948), Smithsonian Folkways boxed set 50068/71 includes both songs.

Lead Belly's unaccompanied singing expresses a prisoner's emotional plea for release. "Old Hannah" was the prisoners' name for the sun which beat down mercilessly as they toiled.

(Ain't Going Down to the Well No More)
Ohhh,
Ain't going down, ain't going down, oh baby,
to the well no more.

Here's a true believer, here's a true believer, yay.
Ain't going down, ain't going down, oh momma,
to the well no more.

If I ever get able, if I ever get able, able to pay this debt I owe, oh,
Ain't going down, ain't going down, oh Sadie,
to the well no more.

Here's a true believer, here's a true believer, yay.
Ain't going down, ain't going down, oh baby,
to the well no more.

Oh, soon one morning when I could not lay back down,
lay back down, oh,
Looking right at her, looking right at her, oh,
standing in her morning gown, oh. (2)

(additional verses)
Oh, down, down in the bottom, mmn.
Mud up to my knees, mud up to my knees, oh Mary,
he was so hard to please.
Oh baby, oh black gal, oh black gal, black gal.

Oh, something funny, oh Lord, Lord, Lord.
I couldn't understand, I couldn't understand,
oh couldn't understand.
Got me charged with murder, got me charged with murder, murder, oh Lord, I ain't raised my hand.
Ain't raised my hand, ain't raised my hand,
oh ain't raised my hand.
Oh black gal, oh black gal, oh.

Turn me loose, turn me loose, please man,
won't you turn me loose?
Lord, I was on the outside, on the outside looking in, oh.
Looking in, looking in, oh black woman, I was looking in.
Now I'm on the inside, Lord, I'm on the inside, inside, oh.

I ain't got no friends, ain't got no friends, praise God,
I ain't got no friends.
Oh Mamie, Petey, come home to the baby, oh.
To the baby, to the baby, oh black gal, to the baby.

(Go Down, Old Hannah)
Go down old Hannah, don't you rise no more,
And if you rise in the morning, bring Judgment Day.

*You oughta been on the Brazos, nineteen and ten.**
Well, they were driving the women like they do the men.

Oh, the sun was shining and the men was flying,
Oh, the captain was hollering and the men was flying.

(additional verses)
If a man don't know, if a man don't know —
*It's a man lying dead on the low turn row.***

Oh, the man on the end hollering
"Bring 'em, bring 'em on in."

It was soon one morning when the sun did rise
And I was singing about my goodlooking baby;
I would hang my head and cry.

Yes, I run to the captain and I shake his hand,
I says, "Look-a here, captain, you got a hardworking man."

Go down old Hannah, don't you rise no more,
If you do rise in the morning, set this world on fire
(change this world around).

And I told the captain that old Ben was dead
And the captain didn't do nothing but nod his head.

Yes, when I went to school, teacher ask me one thing,
She says to me, "Partner, did your mama learn you to sing?"
Then I says, "Go down old Hannah,
I'd like to be knocking on somebody's door."

* Brazos River was the location of state prison farms. 1910 refers to the days of the convict lease system.

** Where teams with ploughs can be turned at the end of the field.

Ain't Going Down To The Well No More/Go Down, Old Hannah

Huddie Ledbetter

edited by John A. Lomax and Alan Lomax

oh soon one morn- ing when I could not lay- back down lay back
down oh ah oh look- ing right at her look- ing right at her oh
stand- ing in her morn- ing gown oh ah oh look- ing right at her
look- ing right at her stand- ing in her morn- ing gown
Go down old Han- nah don't you
rise no more and if you rise in the morn- ing
bring judge- ment day You ought- a been on the
Bra- zos nine- teen and ten well they were
driv- ing the wo- men like they do the men

Alphabetical Song Index